GREENING THE CHRISTIAN
MILLENNIUM

Seán McDonagh SSC

Greening the
Christian
Millennium

DOMINICAN PUBLICATIONS

First published (1999) by
Dominican Publications
42 Parnell Square
Dublin 1

ISBN 1-871552-72-9

British Library Cataloguing in Publications Data.
A catalogue record for this book is available
from the British Library.

Cover design by Bill Bolger

Printed in Ireland by
ColourBooks Ltd, Baldoyle, Dublin 13.

Contents

Catholics and the global environmental crisis

The power unleashed during the twentieth century by the new electrical, chemical, nuclear and biological revolution began to inflict enormous damage in the fabric of life on earth. Every eco-system in every part of the globe has been affected, some more severely than others. The damage everywhere is grave; in a number of situations, like the extinction of species, it is irreversible.

In October 1999, Klaus Topfer, executive director of the UN environment programme, presented an assessment of the future for both humans and the planet when he published *Global Environment Outlook 2000*. It was a devastating indictment of what humans, especially First World people and the élite in the Third World, have done to the planet during the past half-century. The report argued that the main threats to human survival are posed by water shortages, global warming and nitrogen pollution. Land degradation has eroded the fertility of soils across the globe undermining the ability to produce more food for a growing population. In October 1999 it was estimated that 6 billion people lived on the planet. This constitutes an increase of one billion over the 1990 figure. Tropical deforestation had already gone too far. According to Topfer 'a series a looming crises and ultimate catastrophe can only be averted by a massive increase in political will'.

How does one generate that political will? The problem is that very few people in politics, the academic world, industry, finance or the Church really appreciate the magnitude of the crises outlined by Topfer or the urgency with which they must be faced. There are various reasons for this. Each new report of environmental damage is often seen in isolation and thus the cumulative and global impact of what is happening can easily be missed.

In addition there is often a time lag between environmentally destructive activity, like burning fossil fuel, and the moment when the resultant climate change is evident. It is easy to see why environmental issues are often put on the long finger while attention and resources are directed to what are considered more immediate problems like unemployment, social exclusion, racism or poor housing.

It is also true that many are seduced by what might be termed the bright side of technology. It has provided unprecedented comforts, improved medical science, transport, better housing and an array of gadgets for many in the First World during the past few decades. These past achievements and even future promises are so alluring that few wished to count either the social or ecological cost. It was and, to a certain extent, still is easy, especially in First World countries, to be carried along by belief in progress and miss the wider picture, since the degradation oftentimes is not very evident. Satanic mills are no longer pumping black smoke into the sky. But the chemical pollution, the extinction of species and soil erosion, though not as obvious, is more deadly.

It is a tragedy that the Catholic Church, despite its good record on social justice, was one of the last global institutions to address the gravity of the ecological problems now facing the planet. The first and only document from papal magisterium exclusively on this subject appeared only in 1990. In *Peace with God the Creator, Peace with All Creation*, Pope John Paul II states that 'Christians in particular, realize that their responsibility within creation and their duty towards nature and the Creator are an essential part of their faith' (n. 15). The problem is that very few Catholics, including bishops, priests and religious, have ever heard of the document never mind taking its contents to heart. Regularly in talks on ecology and religion I have often quoted this text and asked who wrote it? Very seldom has anyone attributed it to the Pope. Most of the audience who, by and large, would be socially concerned and well educated Catholics have never heard of the document. All, on the other hand, would have heard of *Humanae Vitae*. Catholic teaching on marriage and sexuality is much better known than Catholic teaching on ecology.

The simple fact is that, despite the magnitude and urgency of this issue, ecology is not close to the top of the agenda for Church leaders or Catholics in general. The only place where it is beginning to assume its proper prominence is in the catechetical programmes. Still, it is fair to say that the leadership in the Church has not grappled with this issue in a way that would help build political will in favour of a more sustainable future. Many Church leaders, in recent times, have turned their attention towards 'Churchy' concerns. According to Cardinal König 'they busy themselves with self-criticism and attempts at structural reform'.[1] We seem to have forgotten that the mission of the Church is not to build itself up and tend its own structural needs, but rather be a witness of God's love for the life of the world, *pro mundi vita*.

But even in Cardinal König's reckoning the Church's salvific function is limited to humans. The Churches, he says, 'must be credible interpreters, witnesses of God's love for mankind'. The larger earth context, despite the fact that it is under such great threat, is simply forgotten. The same is true of *Tionól 2000*, one of the initiatives the Irish Church has undertaken to prepare for the millennium. In the 1998 gathering ecology had a very tentative place way out on the margins of the two-day event. It seems to have disappeared altogether from the 1999 gathering. What an oversight! Reclaiming our environment right across the land would be a wonderful target for millennium project. It is would be an opportunity for the Church to re-engage the energies of the young since they are usually concerned about our deteriorating environment. And we are at an environmental cross-roads in Ireland. Even the Irish Environmental Protection Agency in its 1998 report concedes that Ireland's environmental problems are intensifying with economic growth. Forty per cent of the ground water of the country is contaminated with e-coli bacteria. Rivers and lakes like Lough Derg and Lough Rea on the Shannon are polluted with agricultural, human and industrial waste. Household waste has increased by 60 per cent in the past decade and there is nowhere to put it.[2] Agricultural practices, destruction of hedge rows and thoughtless building programmes have silenced birds like larks, yellowhammers, corn buntings and corncrakes that brought joy to the hearts of previous generations of Irish people. The fields are still green but that is as a result of increased fertilizer use and the ubiquitous rye grass.

It is not that these people are opposed to linking ecology with Christian faith. Far from it; once you mention the link everyone agrees that it is important. However, in practice it barely appears in our theology, liturgy or pastoral practice. As far as I know the only bishop in Ireland who has reflected on local and global environmental problems in the light of the millennium is Bishop Murphy of Kerry.[3] Other bishops and bishops' con-ferences have written about the environment. The Philippine Bishops were the first on the scene with the pastoral, *What Has Happened to Our Beautiful Land?* in 1988. They were followed by a statement from the Bishops of Northern Italy. The Guatemalan Bishops have also responded to 'the cry of the land'. The US bishops began their reflection on the environment with a statement in 1991.[4] Unfortunately the majority of local Churches, including the Irish Church, have not produced pastorals on the destruction of God's creation.

If one takes that opening vision of the Vatican II Constitution on the Church in the Modern World as one's guide, concern for the wounded earth should a fundamental concern of Catholics today: 'the joys, and hopes, the grief and anguish of people of our times, especially of those who are poor or afflicted are the joys and hopes, the grief and anguish of the followers of Christ as well' (n. 1).

It was as a response to this aspiration that my own journey in this area began. In the late 1970s I began to work as a missionary among the T'boli people in South Cotabato in the Philippines. There I witnessed at first hand the utter devastation of tropical deforestation and its appalling impact on the land and the people. The more I began to see what was happening to the land, rivers, lakes, coral reefs and mangroves forest the more surprised I was that the Church was silent on the question. At the time the Philippine Church was very vocal, often at great cost to individuals, about human rights abuses and justice. But it had nothing to say about the destruction of God's creation.

I began to speak out about environmental destruction and soon was encouraged to write about the Christian faith and the destruction of the earth. For many it was an unusual subject. Ecology and theology, like oil and water, didn't mix. It took a number of years before any publisher would publish *To Care for the Earth*. In that book I tried to outline the nature of the global environmental stress and argue that it should a major concern for Christians. A few years later *The Greening of the Church* appeared. This looked at some ecological and justice issues e.g. tropical deforestation and the pressure of growing human population levels on the environment. While *To Care for the Earth* had attempted to ground contemporary environmental initiatives in an evolutionary, cosmic story, *The Greening of the Church* looked at what the Bible had to say about ecology. In the mid-1990s *Passion for the Earth* was published. It examined the impact of global economic factors and institutions on the poor and the exploited earth and at how to move concern for the earth to centre stage of the Church's pastoral ministry, especially in the celebration of the sacraments. There is surely no better way in the Catholic tradition of putting people in touch with the sacredness of the earth than by taking the material dimension of sacramental celebrations seriously. How can we baptise people and receive them into a life-giving community with industrial, polluted water?

Greening the Christian Millennium follows a similar pattern. It strives to link environmental concerns with the Christian faith. The book grw out of articles I wrote during the past four eyars for the Dominican journal *Doctrine and Life*. Chapter 1 interprets the life and meaning of Jesus in the context of the widespread destruction of creation. I argue that the gospels support a 'green' vision of Jesus. Our primary affirmation as Christians is that in Jesus God became part of the human and earth condition. The incarnation gives a special dignity not just to the human beings but to the earth and whole cosmos. Furthermore, Christians who are working for justice and a more sustainable world will find inspiration and support in reflecting on the person, ministry and role of Christ in creation. Chapter 2 looks at the devastating impact of Third World Debt on the poor of the earth and the environment and argues that the millennium should be marked by 'Cancelling Unpayable Third World Debts'. Many can take heart from the fact that the pressure to really address this issue has intensified during the autumn of 1999. Much more still needs to be done. In *Peace with God the Creator, Peace with All Creation*, Pope John Paul observes that 'the "green-house" effect has now reached crisis proportions'. Chapter 3 reflects on this global ecological problem in the light of Christian faith. Chapter 4 looks at how humans have treated the oceans as sewers. 'God Called the Waters Seas and Saw That

It Was Good' is a call to protect the very womb of life itself – the seas, rivers and oceans of our world. Power and energy are central to our modern, industrial society. How do we generate this power in a safe and non-polluting way? 'We All Live Downwind from Hiroshima and Chernobyl' (Chapter 5) argues that we should extinguish the nuclear fires before they engulf us. On October 30th a very serious accident took place in a uranium reprocessing plant inn Tokaimura, near Tokyo, Japan. Nuclear accidents do not just happen in former communist countries. They happen in highly industrialised countries with very sophisticated technologies.

New environmental issue arise from new technologies. There is no doubt that the genetic revolution will have profound implications for humans and the earth in the twenty-first century. This new technology needs to be thoroughly assessed from a variety of perspectives before it is released into the environment. 'Ethics and Genetic Engineering' discusses the need for a wider ethical focus for discussing the impact of such new technologies on human health and the well-being of the Earth. It also contends that the scramble in recent years by transnational corporations to patent living organisms has the potential to initiate a new, more pernicious form of dependency between the rich, powerful corporate world in the North and the poor in the South. Finally, 'Eucharist: Renewing the Covenant' argues that the Eucharist which we celebrate each Sunday is pregnant with all kinds of possibilities for deepening our awareness of the holy communion which unites God, humankind, other creatures and all creation. The Eucharist also embodies that mutually enhancing relationship between humans and the rest of creation. The gifts we offer are 'fruit of the earth and work of human hands'. The food that is blessed, broken and shared will sustain us in the challenging task of building a more fair, justice and ecologically sustainable world.

CHAPTER ONE

A Green Christology

'I have come that they may have life
and have it to the full.' (John 10:10)

The offices of environmental organizations may not be the most efficient places in the world, but I am always impressed by the passion and commitment of those working there and the creativity embodied in the posters and cartoons that festoon the walls and, even, the ceiling. Yet as a Catholic missionary, I find it very significant and sad that, whilst the text on the posters might come from Chief Seattle's address or the Indian poet Tagore, I have never seen a quotation from the Bible or a reference to the words of Jesus. It often transpires that many of the people working in these offices promoting campaigns as diverse as biodiversity, organic farming or water conservation are dedicated Christians, but it seems that very little inspiration for their work flows either from the teachings of the Church or the life of Jesus. This is a tragedy, especially for the Christian Churches, because it means that the Good News of Jesus appears to have nothing to contribute to addressing the most crucial issue of the turn of the millennium, the rampant and, often irreversible, destruction of God's creation.

It is particularly tragic because Christians and others have much to learn from the attitude of respect which Jesus displayed towards the natural world. For example, there is no support in the New Testament for an exploitative, throwaway consumer society which in the last four decades has destroyed the natural world in so many parts of the globe and produced mountains of non-biodegradable and toxic waste which will plague the people and creatures of planet Earth for centuries. In the New Testament the disciples of Jesus are called upon to live lightly on the earth – 'take nothing for your journey, no staff, nor bag, nor bread, nor money; and do not have two tunics' (Lk 9:1-6). Jesus constantly warned about the dangers of attachment to wealth, possessions, or power. The forces which are impoverishing hundreds of millions of people in the Third World, and at the same time destroying the planet, very often spring from greed and the allure of mammon. 'How hard it is for those who have riches to enter the kingdom of God' (Mk 10:23; Lk 16:19-31; see Mt 19:23-24; Lk 18:18-23). 'Fool! This very night the demand will be made for your soul; and this hoard of yours, whose will it be then?' (Lk 12:16-21).

Jesus grew up in a rural environment and had an intimacy and familiarity with a variety of God's creatures and the processes of nature. It is clear from his teaching that he was not driven by any urge to dominate or control either his fellow human beings or the world of nature. Rather he displayed an appreciative and contemplative attitude towards creation which was rooted in his Father's love for all creation. "Think of the ravens. They do not sow or reap; they have no storehouses and no barns; yet God feeds them' (Lk 12:24 – NJB). The gospels warn against the urge to continually accumulate more and more goods. God will provide for our legitimate needs: 'are you not worth more than the birds?' (Lk 12:24).

Nature played an important role in Jesus' life. At his birth, Luke tells us that 'he was laid in a manger, because there was no place for them in the inn' (Lk 2:7). Pious tradition has immortalized this in the crib which appears in many Christian homes and churches during the Christmas season. Mary, Joseph and the animals surround Jesus at his birth. He was first greeted by people who were 'keeping watch over their flocks by night' (Lk 2:8). Mark tells us that the Spirit drove him into the wilderness. 'And he was in the wilderness forty days, tempted by Satan; and he was with the wild beasts; and the angels ministered to him'

(Mk 1:13 – RSV).

It was during his sojourn in the desert that Jesus came to accept and appreciate the messianic ministry he was about to embrace. In order to be fully open and receptive to his call, Jesus forsook the company of people and spent time with the wild animals in the wilderness. He regularly returned to the hills to pray and commune with the Father (Mt 17:1; Mk 6:46; Mt 14:23), especially before making important decisions like choosing the disciples (Lk 6:12). His teaching ministry was carried out not so much in buildings, in synagogues or in the temple, as in the cathedral of nature. In Matthew's Gospel the beatitudes and subsequent teachings are delivered on a mountain (Mt 5:1-7:29). Much of his teaching and miracles took place on the shores of the Sea of Galilee (Mt 13:1-52; Mk 4:35-41; Jn 21:1-14). The miracle of the loaves occurred in a 'lonely place' (Mt 14:15-21; Lk 9:10-17; Jn 6:1-13).

Many of his parables are centred on nature: He speaks of sowing seed (Mt 13:4-9, 18-23; Mk 4:3-9, 13-20; Lk 8:5-8, 11-15), of vines (Jn 5:1-1-17; Mk 12:1-12; Mt 21:33-44; Lk 20:9-19), the lost sheep (Lk 15:4-7; Mt 18:12-14), or the life and work of shepherds (Jn 10:1-18). His teaching is regularly interspersed with references to the lilies of the field (Lk 12:27), the birds of the air (Mt 6:26), and the lair of foxes (Lk 9:58). He was Lord of creation and could calm the waves (Mk 4:35-41; Mt 8:22-25), or walk on the water (Mk 6:48-49), or, when food was needed, multiply the loaves (Mt14:13-21; Mk 8:1-10; Lk 9:10-17; Jn 6:1-13).

Jesus was a healer. He cured the sick and restored them to health (Mt 12:9-14; Mk 3:1-6; Lk 6:6-11). He cured the paralytic (Mk 2:1-12), the man with a withered hand (Mk 3:1-6), the woman who had been stooped for many years (Lk 13:10-17), and the man who had been paralysed for thirty-eight years (Jn 5:1-15). H restored sight to the man born blind (Jn 9:1-41). The healing ministry of Jesus was not confined to individuals. Each healing was a sign that challenged social or religious prejudices, and also aimed at sowing a seed of healing within a community which was attempting to open itself up to the transforming power of God's compassion and graciousness.

In his preaching also Jesus identified himself with the natural elements of water (Jn 4:13-14), bread (Jn 6:48) and light (Jn 8:12). He presented himself as the good shepherd (Jn 10:11; Mk 6:30-44) who came that 'they may have life and have it abundantly' (Jn 10:10b). He rode into Jerusalem on a donkey (Mt 21:1b-5). In Mark's Gospel (16:15) the disciples were called to take the gospel to *all creation*. Finally in and through his death, Jesus participated in the most radical way in one of the key processes of nature.

The ministry of Jesus was not confined to teaching, healing and reconciling humans and all creation with God. His life and ministry had a cosmic dimension. Paul tells us that he is the centre of all creation.

> He is the image of the invisible God, the first-born of all creation; for in him all things were created, in heaven and on earth, visible and invisible, whether thrones or dominions or principalities or authorities – all things were created through him and for him. He is before all things, and in him all things hold together. (Col 1:15-8 – RSV).

Jesus is the word and wisdom of God who existed with God from the beginning. In the prologue of John's gospel the birth and life of Jesus are framed within the widest context of cosmic history. He is active in bringing forth creation; through him the universe, the earth and all life was created (Jn 1:3-5). All the rich unfolding of the universe from the first moment of the fireball, through the formation of the stars, the moulding of planet earth, the birth and flowering of life on earth and the emergence of human beings, is centred on Christ. Hence all these crucial moments in the emergence of the universe have a Christic dimension.

In the man Jesus, God who was active from the beginning in bringing forth the universe 'became flesh' (Jn 1:14). The Greek word which is used here (*sarx*) has a very earthy ring to it. Scholars believe that the author consciously chose this word to attack the Gnostic teaching which was prevalent at the time. For Gnostics, *sarx* was evil and could not in any way be co-mingled with the Divine. In the face of this the author of the Gospel of John insists that Jesus enters into every dimension of earthly reality. The redemption which he accomplishes does not come by way of discarding, denigrating or abandoning *sarx*, but by transforming *sarx* from within. In John 3:16, Jesus' incarnation is seen as an outpouring of God's love for the world – 'for God so loved the world that he gave his only Son, that whoever believes in him should not perish but have eternal life' (RSV).

Christ's life of service involved a radical stance on the side of life, which necessitated his own suffering and death. He atoned for sins against life (Heb 9:12). Paul presents Jesus' incarnation in this light in Phil 2:5-7 and Col 1:15-20.

> Make your own the mind of Christ Jesus;
> Who, being in the form of God,
> did not count equality with God
> something to be grasped.
> But he emptied himself,
> taking the form of a slave,
> becoming as human beings are. (Phil 2:5-7 – NJB)

The leadership which Jesus gives in the New Testament is always a leadership of service. When an argument broke out among the disciples as to which of them was the greatest, Jesus admonished them;

Among the gentiles it is the kings who lord it over them and those who have authority over them are given the title Benefactor. With you this must not happen. No, the greatest among you must believe as if he were the youngest, the leader as if he were the one who serves. (Lk 22:25-26 – NJB)

This leadership involved accepting death joyfully. Paul in Philippians goes on to say:

And being in every way like a human being,
he was humbler yet,
even to accepting death, death on a cross (Phil 2:6-8 – NJB)

A service which involves emptying oneself and working for the good of others is at the very heart of the Christian vocation. The follower of Christ does not seek power and riches in order to manipulate other human beings and beggar the earth. Rather he/she hears the call: 'if anyone wants to be a follower of mine, let him renounce himself and take up his cross every day and follow me' (Lk 9:23). In the contemporary situation, Christian service must mean working for a more just world and preserving the earth. This call to serve all creation throws a new light on the Genesis call to 'be masters of the fish of the sea, the birds of heaven and all living creatures that move on earth' (Gen 1:26). In following Christ's example this 'dominion' includes a deep respect for the ecological laws which bind creation together; the kind of care that Noah displayed when he took the animals into the ark (Gen 6:19). Only in this way can people of this and future generations experience the abundant life which Jesus promised (Jn 10:10).

The passion and death of Christ call attention to the appalling reality of suffering which humans inflict on each other and on creation. By causing others to suffer we persecute the body of Christ. We are beginning to realise that the parameters of the body of Christ are expanding to include not just Christians or all humans, but the totality of creation. Paul was reminded on the road to Damascus that in persecuting the Christians he was persecuting Jesus (Acts 9:4-5). In today's world many see the passion of Christ being re-enacted in the injustices which are inflicted on the weak and the poor, in cruelty to animals and in the devastation which humans are wreaking on creation. This pain experienced by the total body of Christ is captured in a prayer from the Byzantine liturgy: 'The whole creation was altered by thy Passion; for all things suffered with thee, knowing, O Lord, that thou holdest all things in unity'.

Jesus' life shows us how to live our own life to the full in the face of the mystery of death. By facing death he achieved glorification. Paul again confesses, 'therefore God highly exalted him and bestowed on him the name which is above every name, that at the name of Jesus every knee should bow, in heaven and on earth and under the earth, and every tongue confess that Jesus Christ is Lord, to the glory of God' (Phil 2:9-11 – RSV). Many contemporary psychologists believe that the frenzied grasping for more and more possessions which lies at the root of our consumer society arises primarily out of our anxieties in the face of our own death. By surrounding ourselves with more and more goods we hope to avoid the reality of death and gain some measure of immortality, at least, in the things that we own.

The New Testament tells us that this resistance to death is a blind alley. The tragedy for ourselves, the human community and creation as a whole, is that in pursuing this illusion, individually and collectively, we are destroying irreversibly God's creation – the air, the water, the soil, the forests and the abundance of life-forms.

In seeking to avoid death, we are literally killing planet earth. This is why Jesus' way of living his life into death, trusting completely in the love of his Father, must become the foundational reality in our lives. His death, and especially his resurrection, is the basis of our hope that we can turn back the tide of planetary death.

The resurrection of Christ is the beginning of the new creation (2 Cor 5:17-19). All the writers of the New Testament are at pains to affirm the visible, bodily nature of Christ's resurrection. They are not professing that an immortal spirit put on the guise of a human body in order to be present to his disciples and others. The Greeks would have found such a concept very acceptable, not folly. The evangelists are adamant that he rose in the flesh (Mt 28:1-8; Mk 16:1-8; Lk 24:1-10; Jn 20:1-10). This corporeal nature of Christ's resurrection came as a complete surprise for the disciples and the early Church. So the writers of the New Testament are at pains to stress the bodily dimension of his resurrection. They do this by recounting a variety of incidents where Jesus touched people (Jn 20:27) and ate with them (Jn 21:4-14). In his resurrection Jesus was transformed in his total person, which naturally affected his body. His resurrected body is no longer confined by its previous limitations. He can pass easily through solid substances and visit his disciples who because of their fear are huddled together in an upper room on the evening of the resurrection (Jn 20:19).

Through the reality of Christ's resurrection all visible created reality is touched, given new significance and transformed. Paul states: 'God was in Christ reconciling the world to himself' (2 Cor 5:19, Col 1:20). In this text Paul is affirming that all reality is both interconnected, sequentially linked over time and ultimately grounded in God. The Easter Preface in the Roman Liturgy echoes this belief: 'In him a new age has dawned, the long reign of sin is ended, a broken world has been renewed and man is once again made whole. The joy of the resurrection fills the whole world'.

The resurrection is the cosmic sign of hope. All creation is united in Christ and therefore everything has a future in God, through Christ. This hope for wholeness or redemption is anchored in the presence in the world of the Spirit of God, who despite human failures and sin, can bring about new beginnings (Is 43:19, Ezek 37). This grace frees the believer to look forward confidently to the future and not to be bogged down in either individual or collective past failures. This is a profoundly liberating experience which can release new energies and allow people to focus their attention on bringing about a healing of creation.

In recent years it is beginning to dawn on many people that alleviating, healing nature and preserving the stability of the biosphere is the central task for those who wish to follow in the footsteps of Jesus in today's world. Human creativity, inventiveness and technology will have a very important part to play in this healing, but religious energies flowing from the life, death and resurrection of Jesus are also crucial. In the words of the Celtic hymn, 'Christ Be beside Me', based on St. Patrick's *Breastplate*, Christ can surely be the vision of those who are working at local, national and global level to create a new heavens and a new earth.

CHAPTER TWO

Cancelling Unpayable Third World Debts

During the summer of 1998 much of the financial news and analysis in the media dealt with the ailing tiger economies in Asia, the collapsing Russian ruble, the near bankruptcy of the Long-Term Capital Markets Hedge Funds and wild swings in stock markets. How did it happen? Could the collapse of these economies lead to a global depression and drag down the economies of the North? Such questions were debated on talk-shows and in newspaper columns. Yet amid all this talk it seems that the Third World Debt crisis that came to a head in the early 1980s and is which is still impoverishing the poorest of the poor in our world and destroying their environment, has been forgotten. In 1980 the debt was $600 billion. In 1999 it now stands at approximately $2.2 trillion despite the fact that in the intervening twenty years these countries have paid hundreds of billions of dollars servicing the debts.

Some of the world's media did call for the cancellation of the debts of the four countries in Central America which were devastated by hurricane Mitch in late October 1998. The storm killed at least 24,000 people. Two million were left homeless. Roads, bridges and the power and telecommunication grid were destroyed. Erosion destroyed agricultural land and wiped out many banana plantations and left tens of thousands of people without jobs. Many commentators estimate that given the scale of the destruction it will take Honduras at least 20 years to recover from the effects of the storm. Any possibility of recovery will be severely hampered if these countries have to go on paying their external debts. Between them, El Salvador, Honduras, Nicaragua, and Costa Rica pay £3 million dollars a day servicing their debts.

In the wake of Mitch the governments of these countries

pleaded with the international community to cancel their debts. The industries that provided their foreign exchange have been destroyed so that the countries are not able to meet the interest payments on their loans. Britain and France have called for a three year moratorium on debt payments.

Many of the actors involved, including governments and aid agencies, know that a moratorium is not sufficient. In December 1998 the Honduran ambassador to Britain, Roberto Flores Bermudez, put the case for debt cancellation forcefully. 'Honduras has no revenue to pay for both its debts and its reconstruction, not because of bad policies or because it doesn't wish to, but because the capacity was mortally crushed by a force majeure'.[1] All major sources of foreign exchange – bananas, shrimp-farming, coffee and sugar plantations and melon-growing – have all been severely disrupted. Seventy percent of the productive infrastructure of Honduras was destroyed by the storm . Unfortunately, in December 1998 finance ministers and officials from First World countries meeting at the Paris Club refused to cancel Central American debt and opted instead for a three year moratorium.

The development prospects of other countries in Africa, Asia and Latin America are also being undermined by the burden of debt payments. In the past two decades servicing this debt has entailed haemorrhaging of hundreds of billions of dollars from poor people in the South to the affluent North. In her book, *The Debt Boomerang*, Susan George estimates that between 1982 and 1990 there was a net transfer of $US418 billion from the poor South to the rich North. In order to help people understand the enormous sums involved she writes that it is the equivalent of six Marshall Plans.[2] The Marshall Plan provided much needed aid from the US which was used to rebuild the economies of war-torn Europe after the destruction of World War II. Today, however, money that should be used to alleviate poverty, and preserve the environment in poor countries, is siphoned off to increase the affluence of a small number of people in Northern countries.

The debt burden is crippling the people of Sub-Sahara Africa. In 1962 the countries of that region had a debt of $3 billion. It jumped to a staggering $142 billion in the early 1980s and today it stands at $225 billion. Paying the debt takes scarce resources from health care and education. According to Oxfam, 100,000 Ethiopian children die each year from diseases that are easily preventable. Because the Ethiopian government spends four times more on debt servicing than on health care sickness and death will continue to blight individuals and communities. Things are no better on the educational front in Africa. Only half the school-age population is attending school. Even their educational prospects are not too bright as many of these schools are substandard and the teachers are poorly educated. Everyone involved in development work knows that there cannot be a bright future without investment in education. But such investment cannot happen when four times more is paid to Northern creditors than is spent on basic education.[3]

The frightening thing about the treadmill of debt is that the amount owed grows even after such savage financial blood letting. In the early 1990s the Philippines laboured under the weight of a US$29 billion foreign and $9 billion domestic debt. Between the fall of the Marcos dictatorship in 1986 and 1992, during the presidency of Cory Aquino, the country paid $18 billion servicing the foreign debt. Yet by 1992 it had grown by another $3 billion.

The same process was at work in Mexico which was brought to the brink of bankruptcy through debt-related policies in 1982. During the next six years it was forced to scrape together $100 billion in debt servicing yet in 1988, its debt exceeded the original 1982 figure.[4] A similar pattern emerged in Guyana one of the poorest countries in Latin America with a GNP per capita of only $590. When its debt crisis blew up in the early 1980s it owed foreign banks and Northern countries over $2 billion. After almost ten years of severe structural adjustment in which the country's natural resources – wood, bauxite and gold – were sold to foreign companies, spending on education, health and welfare slashed, and $1.7 billion paid out in debt repayments it still owes $1.5 billion. Over half of the debt is made up of accumulated interest and a significant percentage of the money was spent to pay foreign consultants for technical assistance, advice or materials.[5]

How the debt arose

It is important to remember that the Third World debt problem was caused by actions that were taken both in the wealthy countries of the North and in poor Southern countries. The United States spent vast sums of money in the 1960s pursuing a war in South-East Asia. Instead of raising taxes to cover these expenses it simply printed more dollars. This put huge pressure on the dollar that had been linked to the gold standard since the Bretton Woods Conference in 1944. In 1972 President Nixon took the US off the gold standard. This action lowered the value of the US dollar and set in train inflationary pressures.

Further inflationary pressures were swept across the global economy in 1972 when the then Soviet Union purchased the entire US grain surplus. As a result grain prices trebled. In response to this the Organization of Petroleum Exporting Countries (OPEC) decided to raise the price of oil which jumped from $3.50 a barrel to $16.00 in 1973.

The four-fold increase sent huge amounts of money flowing into the coffers of OPEC countries especially in the Middle East. The amounts were so great that some of these countries were unable to absorb all the money for domestic programmes. They deposited the money in US, European and Japanese banks. Awash with petrodollars the banks sought every opportunity to invest the money and, in the process, make a hefty profit. The investment climate was not bright in Northern countries, especially Europe, as increased energy costs had triggered a sharp recession.

Undeterred, the First World banks looked south to the Third World as a favourable location for their investment. Governments in the Third World, urged on by Northern consultants from institutions like the World Bank, judged it a favourable time to borrow. Interest rates were low. Borrowing cheap money seemed to be an eminently reasonable way of undertaking much needed development. In the 1970s the World Bank stated repeatedly that 'there is no general problem of developing countries being able to service debt'.[6]

Unfortunately things went badly wrong. In the early 1980s the foreign debts grew out of control. Some of the blame, undoubtedly, must be laid at the door of Southern politicians and their economic advisers. A huge portion of the borrowed money, as high as 20 per cent according to the International Peace Research Institute in Stockholm, was spent on arms. India and Pakistan between them spend more than $10 billion a year importing arms.

In many situations these imported arms allowed dictators like Suharto to terrorise and murder their own people and still stay in power. Increased weapons sales boosted the profits for the arms industry in the US, Britain, the USSR, France, East Germany and Czechoslovakia – to mention just a few countries. The arms export business was notorious for widespread corruption. It is now estimated that 15 per cent of the Al Yamamah defence contract between Saudi Arabia and the UK, worth £40 billion, went on various forms of commission.

Much of the money was also squandered on grandiose

projects or transferred to foreign bank accounts. In the early 1980s the Philippine government spent over $2.2 billion building a nuclear power plant in Bataan, one of the most geologically active areas in the world. Luckily, the nuclear fire was never started. Nevertheless, the cost of servicing the loan for the Philippine government runs to approximately $200,000 each day.

A lot of the money was also embezzled. It was widely believed in the Philippines that former President Marcos and his wife deposited over $5 billion dollars in Swiss banks. Charges of corruption plagued the building of the Bataan nuclear power plant. The two main contenders for the project were General Electric and Westinghouse corporation. General Electric was in a strong position to land the lucrative contract. In order to wrest the contract for themselves Westinghouse offered a friend and golfing partner of Marcos, Herminio Disini, a 5 per cent commission if he could secure the contract for them. This he duly did. Based on the contract price, this consultancy fee could amount to $80 million. Westinghouse admits paying Disini $17.3 million in cash as a consultant. There is no absolute proof that Marcos got part of the Disini payoff, but there is documentary evidence that Marcos co-owned Disini's business.

Finally, it is worth remembering that the Philippine government and the National Power Corporation of the Philippines would not have been able to enter into such negotiations but for the fact that the US Export-Import Bank provided huge loans despite the problematic nature of tendering.

President Marcos and his wife were not alone in looting their national treasuries. Lopez-Portillo of Mexico, Anastasio Somoza of Nicuragua, ex-President Suharto of Indonesia, the generals in Nigeria, the late President Mobuto of Zaire all enriched themselves with monies borrowed by their countries. Mobuto ran up a foreign debt of $5 billion roughly similar to his own personal wealth.

An organization called Transparency International, which was set up both to monitor corruption in business and aid and campaign against it, has drawn up a hierarchy of most and least corrupt countries. Nigeria heads the corruption list followed by Bolivia, Columbia and Russia. The leaders of these countries stashed away a significant percentage of this borrowed money in Northern banks.

Morgan Guaranty Trust Company did a study of 'capital flight' in the mid-1980s. They estimated that in a single year $198 billion was transferred out of eighteen developing countries to Northern banks. Of that, $31 billion was deposited in US bank accounts. 'The problem', according to a member of the US Federal Reserve, ' is not that Latin Americans don't have assets. They do. The problem is that they're all in Miami'.[7] Much of this money was recycled through commercial banks back to the First World countries from which the loans came in the first place.

Defrauders could not have achieved grand scale larceny had the lending institutions exercised due diligence by checking the credentials of the lender and the economic viability of the projects. 'Know your client' is one of the cardinal rules of banking. The banks chose to disregard this maxim and opted for the newly invented 'syndicated loans'. They relied on the large banks to do the necessary investigations and hoped that they would find some sort of default limitation by spreading the risk among a number of financial institutions.

Because of their complicity in both their lending policies and the way they facilitated capital flight Northern banks and governments must bear huge responsibility for the outcome. They knew that regimes headed by the likes of Mr Marcos were brutal and corrupt. Many of the debts can be considered 'odious debts'. They were contracted by illegally constituted regimes often in violation of the laws of the lending countries. However in the skewed morality of the Cold War such ethical considerations were disregarded and support for right-wing tyrants like Marcos, Pinochet and Suharto posed no dilemma for many Western leaders.

But external factors played an even more central role in creating such appalling mountains of indebtedness. When the borrowing spree began interest rates were low. However, towards the late 1970s and early 1980s interest rates sky-rocketed. In May 1981 the US prime rate peaked at 21.5 per cent. Most of the loans were borrowed at variable rates, pitched approximately one percent above the US prime rate. Driven by such high interest rates Third World debts grew by leaps and bounds. The interests rates during most of the 1980s were simply usurious.

It is worth pointing out that this global hike in interest rates had nothing to do with the internal functioning of the economies of debtor countries. It derived from the fact that the U.S., in an effort to have the rest of the world finance its military and commercial expansion without raising taxes, was forced to raise interest rates to attract inward investment, mostly from Japan and Germany.

While interest rates were going through the ceiling, commodity prices were plummeting through the floor as a result of recession in Europe and North America. The fall in commodity prices was a particularly cruel blow for Third World countries. Most of them were former colonies whose economies had been shaped during the nineteenth and twentieth centuries by their European masters to produce one or two commodities for export. In the mid and late 1970s commodity prices tumbled world-wide. A basket of twenty-eight commodities which included lead, zinc, tin, sugar, coffee and tea was worth 48 per cent less in 1988 than in 1974. This meant that many debtor countries could not accumulate enough foreign exchange to service their debts. Commodity prices are, once again, tumbling in the late 1990s. According to *Newsweek*, since early 1997 prices 'of raw materials (oil, wheat, copper, coffee) have dropped 10 to 40 percent on world markets'.[8]

Structural Adjustment Programmes (SAPs)

In August 1982 Mexico threatened to default on its external debts. If Mexico had defaulted many of the largest US banks, including Citibank and Chase Manhattan, could have tumbled over the precipice into bankruptcy. Forty four per cent of the capital of the nine largest U.S. banks was tied up in Mexican loans. If Mexico defaulted, 44 per cent of their capital would have to be written off, their stocks would have plummeted on the stock-market as shareholders sold out. If other nations followed suit, worldwide financial chaos would have been inevitable. To avoid this happening the World Bank and the International Monetary Fund, acting as debt collector for lending countries and banks, forced economic stabilisation and structural adjustment programmes (SAPs) on Third World countries, beginning with Mexico.

The formula was simple: Earn more and spend less. The details often differed slightly but, in general, they included currency devaluation, cutbacks in government expenditure, an elimination of subsidies and price controls, a drop in wages, opening up to foreign competition and investment, an emphasis on export-oriented industry and agriculture, widespread privatization of government industries leading to lay-offs and increased unemployment. Cutbacks in education, health and social welfare budgets have taken a terrible toll on the well-being of the poor, especially women and children, in Third World countries. The impact of what amounts to economic shock treatment has been so severe and destructive that even the World Bank and the International Monetary Fund have been forced to introduce social safety nets in more recent SAPs.

A few examples will illustrate the pain and destruction which has followed in the wake of the debt crisis. Zambia, a country familiar to many Irish missionaries and development workers which benefits from the Irish government's aid budget, is a good example of how debt can bring a country to its knees. In 1995 Zambia, with a debt of $6.85 billion, was one of the most heavily indebted low income countries in the world. Each Zambian child was born with a debt of £730 hanging over her/ his head. This represents twice the GNP per capita.

In 1964 Zambia achieved political independence from Britain. While the following two decades under the leadership of Kenneth Kaunda were far from perfect, in that effective opposition was stifled through the establishment of a one-party system, many advances were made in education and human well-being. Infant mortality fell from 125 to 80 per thousand births, and life expectancy rose from 41 to 54 years by the mid-1980s. Zambia borrowed heavily in the 1970s and early 1980s to spear-head developments in infrastructure projects. In the late 1980s and 1990s it borrowed to support the economic reform package (SAPs) devised by the World Bank and IMF.

It is true that some aspects of the liberalisation programmes have helped people. In some situation removing controls has helped make more goods available for those who can afford to buy. It has also allowed entrepreneurs to use their initiative to develop small businesses and improve their economy situation. Nevertheless the impact of SAPs and other global economic factors have proved disastrous for Zambia. Copper accounted for 90 per cent of Zambia's foreign exchange earnings in the 1970s. Over-dependence on a single commodity leaves a country very vulnerable to changing economic conditions. Zambia was no exception. In response to technological breakthroughs in fibre optics, copper prices tumbled by 50 per cent on world markets between 1970 and 1990. The fall in demand in turn led to a one third drop in copper production in Zambia during the same period. Starved of foreign exchange with which to service its debts, Zambia has fallen into arrears.

In addition, the borrowing strategies the Zambian government was encouraged to use in the 1980s and 1990s, in supporting structural adjustment programmes, also backfired. Recently the World Bank reviewed eighteen projects that had been approved by the Bank itself in the period between 1980 and 1995. Only three of the projects were judged capable of generating the financial resources necessary to repay the loans within the prescribed period. The sad fact is that Zambia's debt has doubled since 1980 while its GNP has been halved.

The impact of such an economic collapse can be seen in both education and the health services. The burden of servicing the external debt means that money is not available for social, health and educational programmes: between 1990 and 1993 the government of Zambia spent $37 million on primary school education and $1.3 billion on debt repayments. Repayments to the IMF alone amounted to ten times the amount spent on primary education.

In the years after independence Zambia vigorously promoted primary and secondary level education. The debt crisis and subsequent SAPs have taken a heavy toll on education. The education budget declined from 16 per cent in 1984 to 9 per cent in 1992. Even more worrying is the fact that the per capita public spending on primary school students is now one sixth of what it was a decade ago. Structural adjustment programmes forced the government to introduce primary and secondary school fees. These have hit the poor, and especially girls, who have been forced to drop-out of school at a very early age.

There is also a marked decline in the quality of education and in teachers' morale. Salaries have not kept pace with the cost of living. A teacher's monthly salary is around 120,000 Kwacha, while a basket of food for a family of six for April 1997 cost K170,592. There is no money to cover other basic household necessities, clothes or medical expenses. As a result many dedicated teachers have emigrated or sought employment in the private sector. Between 1986 and 1990 almost five thousand Zambian teachers moved to Botswana and South Africa in search of better wages. During a visit to Zambia in September 1998 some of the most dedicated teachers I met told me that, because of poor salaries, they were looking for career opportunities elsewhere in Africa.

The same disintegration is evident in the health services. Chronic malnutrition affects almost half Zambia's children. Infant mortality has climbed from 150 per thousand in the 1980s to 202 per thousand in 1992. Forty per cent of Zambian children are stunted as a result of chronic under-nutrition over an extended period.[9] At the same time, life expectancy has also dropped from 54 in 1990 to 45 in 1994. Access to clean water has also declined with a consequent increase in water-borne diseases like cholera, diarrhoea and malaria. Finally, the number of health personnel, especially doctors, had also dropped from 1 per 7,000 in 1985 to 1 per 13,000 in 1991. Once again, many have migrated to South Africa in search of better wages. User fees have been introduced at hospitals and health centres with a resulting 60 to 80 per cent drop in attendance.[10]

Problems caused by debt and structural adjustment policies are not unique to Zambia or other African countries. The crisis initially came to consciousness in the South and North in the wake of the Mexican debt moratorium in 1982. At that time the Third World debt choked off economic growth, increased poverty in the South and also threatened to drag down many

Northern financial institutions. Both in the North and South it was considered a 'crisis'. Within a few years a combination of stabilisation initiatives and structural adjustment programmes in the South and generous tax breaks in the North eased the pressure on Northern banks. The brutal treatment meted out by the financial institutions led by the IMF to President Alan Garcia of Peru who attempted, unilaterally, to peg his country's debt-service payments at 10 per cent of export earnings served as a warning to other debtor countries who might be planning to follow his example. In 1986 when Peru only paid $370 million out of the $1.5 billion that it owed, the IMF declared Peru ineligible for further loans. The World Bank then halted all disbursements to Peru. The private commercial banks refused credit to Peru, effectively undermining its economy. Within a few years Peru began to pay its loans.

With the stabilisation and structural adjustment policies in place Northern countries and financial institutions breathed a sigh of relief and began to view Third World debt more as a 'problem' rather than a 'crisis'. By the early 1990s the Third World Debt had disappeared from the agenda of the G7 countries. In 1992 *The Economist*, full of naive optimism as a result of its free-market ideology, boldly declared: 'The debt crisis R.I.P'. It proclaimed that 'the banks have put the third-world debt behind them, and some debtors have queues of investors banging at their doors'.[11]

Debt in Latin America

But the impact of the debt is still very real in Latin America and other poor countries. The combined foreign debt of Latin American nations in November 1997 was $600 billion. This amounted to an increase of almost $200 billion since the height of the debt crisis in the mid 1980s. Little wonder that 30 per cent of all export-earnings are now swallowed-up in debt servicing. The knock-on effect is an increase in malnutrition such that diseases like tuberculosis, malaria and cholera, which had shown a marked decline in the 1960s and 1970s, have returned with a vengeance.

One effect of the debt crisis is the increased availability of drugs in the US and Europe. It is now estimated that the complex of anti-drug activities in the US, from financing people in jail to rehabilitation and education services, costs the US taxpayer over $15 billion annually. The link between increased drug trafficking and debt is obvious in Bolivia. This is one of the poorest countries in Latin America with an estimated 70 per cent of the population of its 8 million people living below the poverty line. Until the 1980s the Bolivian economy was dominated by a major commodity – tin mining. In 1985 tin prices tumbled on world markets and the tin industry collapsed. The consequent economic upheaval drove tens of thousands of former miners and their families into the Chapare region of the country which is a well-known cocaine-producing area. Today it is estimated that up to 20 per cent of the work-force, close to 500,000 people, are involved in some way in what is called the macro-economy. These are not just the growers or processors. The police, customs officers and people in the government have to be paid off in order to facilitate cocaine export to the US.

At a meeting in 1990, President Jaime Paz Zamora of Boliva bluntly told the then US President, George Bush, that half of Bolivia's imports were financed by the coca-cocaine trade and that 70 per cent of GDP was cocaine related. The US authorities were attempting to put pressure on the Bolivian government to take a tougher stance against cocaine production. Legislation was introduced to phase out cocaine and compensate the *cocaleros* or coca-growers. The US has allocated $48 million to combat cocaine in Bolivia and facilitate the growing of other crops like pineapples, tea and rice.

These drug-substitution programmes have not been very successful in stopping the flow of drugs. Violence erupts when the police or army raid and burn or destroy cocaine plantations. It is obvious that governments which depend on drug trafficking for foreign exchange will protect or, at least, turn a blind eye to the drugs business, especially when the foreign debt stands at over $5 billion. One of the most effective ways of stemming the flood of cocaine into the US and Europe would be to lift the burden of debt from countries like Bolivia and Peru. According to Emma Donlan of Christian Aid: 'Bolivia's ability to unlock the potential for economic growth is being undermined by the unbearable burden of debt which diverts 30 per cent of the country's income to rich creditor countries and the international financial institutions. Any anti-drug programme in Bolivia must accept the need for substantial debt reduction now'.[12]

Given the impact of debt in Latin America it is little wonder that foreign debt was a recurring theme at the Synod of the Americas that took place in Rome in November 1997. In his presentation Archbishop Antonio Jose Gonzalez Zumarraga of Quito, Ecuador described its impact on his country.

Ecuador is a small country of 275,000 sq. km. of territorial surface with 12 million inhabitants. If one distributes the public debt to each inhabitant, each of the Ecuadorians would have to pay $1,200 ... If one considers that 60 or 70 per cent of the Ecuadorian population is poor, one comes to the conclusion that Ecuador cannot materially pay its external debt with the contribution of its own inhabitants ...

The drain that debt servicing has put on the national budget has grown over the years and is now very substantial. In 1988 the figure was 12 per cent. It jumped to 27 per cent in 1989 and by 1996 it was eating up 36.05 per cent. In 1997, 30 per cent of the budget or 18 billion Ecuadorian sucres was allotted to servicing the external debt. This means that the

State will not be able to allocate sufficient funds for education, which, by law, must receive 30 per cent of the budget;
however, it will get only 21.19 per cent, and health will get
barely 3 or 4 per cent of the national budget. The lack of
sufficient attention to public education causes periodic strikes
by educators to the detriment of the education of children
and youth. There are frequent strikes by family doctors and
health workers, who demand not only higher salaries, but,
above all, more attention to public hospitals. These strikes,
including those of governmental sectors, frequently disturb
civil peace and social order.[13]

The debt is costing the earth

The debt crisis has destroyed the environment in many Third
World countries. Many loans, even those from the World Bank,
financed ecologically destructive projects. For years the Bank
simply ignored environmental considerations and proceeded
to fund dams, hydroelectric and irrigation projects, many of
which had lamentable environmental consequences.

In *Mortgaging the Earth* Bruce Rich examines a number of
these projects which turned out to be social and environmental
disasters. Two Brazilian projects – Carajas (a mining, smelting
and railway development) and Polonoroeste (road building
and agricultural colonisation) – are particularly destructive.
Despite the historical fact that previous efforts to colonise the
Amazon had failed dismally and the Bank's own Operations
Evaluation Department (OED) had raised serious doubts about
the viability of the project, hundreds of millions of dollars were
poured into the Polonoroeste project in the 1980s. Rich writes
that Polonoroeste 'transformed Rodonia – an area approximately the size of Oregon or Great Britain – into a region with
one of the highest forest destruction rates in the Brazilian
Amazon'.[14]

The Carajas project had a similar impact on the tropical forest, at the other end of the Amazon basin, in the state of Para. Here the World Bank lent over £300 million in order to build a railway to transport high-grade ore to the sea. Included in the original project were plans to build thirty-four charcoal-burning industries to produce pig iron along the railway corridor. Timber for charcoal was supposed to come from eucalyptus plantations. In fact it came from the standing forests and this has resulted in massive deforestation in the area.

Export-orientated economic policies, driven by structural adjustment programmes, have stimulated an increase in the exploitation of natural resources, including the extraction of minerals, tropical hard woods and cash crops. Senegal borrowed heavily to buy expensive machinery to process a million tonnes of groundnuts. However, constant mono-cropping with groundnuts has so depleted the soil that the one million tonnes target will not be reached. Nevertheless the cost of the machinery must be repaid.

Debt repayments has increased tropical forest destruction. In Brazil the Amazon forest has been burnt each year to facilitate beef production which is destined for fast-foods outlets globally. In Guyana most of the forests that covers 70 per cent of the country have been sold off in an effort to raise foreign currency to pay the external debt. Forest burning is also rampant in South East Asia.

In other tropical areas like the Philippines the widespread poverty which has followed in the wake of SAPs has driven millions of poor, landless people into the rainforests in search of land on which to eke out an existence. Susan George reproduces a chart showing that the majority of the top debtor countries like Brazil and Mexico have increased their levels of deforestation significantly in the 1970s and 1980s. The increase in Brazil is by a whopping 245 per cent.[15]

I experienced directly the impact of tropical deforestation on a tribal community and their lands during my twelve years living among a tribal people called the T'boli in a remote part of Southern Mindanao in the Philippines. The mountains were eroded, topsoil was lost and it was generally agreed that the removal of forest cover had a negative effect on the local climate.

Debt-related ecological destruction adds to global warming, the extinction of species and erosion

Tropical deforestation is a tragedy for those who live in or depend on the forest for their livelihood. But the chain of desolation extends far beyond the tropics and touches the whole planet. At the Kyoto meeting on global warming in December 1997 many contributors highlighted the correlation between forest destruction and global warming. This is a global phenomenon that will harm the lives of future generations, especially those living in coastal areas and in low-lying islands in the Pacific. It will also disrupt weather patterns. Many climatologists believe that the ferocity of hurricane Mitch was related to changes brought about by global warming. Changes in rainfall patterns in places like the great plains of North America would increase world hunger. Susan George quotes the botanist Norman Myers who estimates that 'around 18 or 19 per cent' of the increase in greenhouse gases during the past two decades is due to tropical deforestation.

The greatest loss for future generations, mainly because it is irreversible, is the horrendous fact of extinction. It is estimated that tens of thousands of species have become extinct through deforestation. Even though tropical forests only occupy approximately 6 per cent of the world's land area, they are estimated to contain over half the species in the world. That is why the destruction of rainforests is such a catastrophe.

Writing in 1992, the Harvard biologist, Dr Edward Wilson summed up the cumulative effect of forest plunder in the Philippines during the post-war era: 'this island nation is at the edge of a full-scale biodiversity collapse'.[16] Many of the estimated 80,000 species of plants found in Philippine forests are highly nutritious and could easily be added to the larder of staple foods in the Philippines and beyond its frontiers. Extinction means that this rich potential for new sources of food and medicine will never come to fruition.

The saga of death that follows in the wake of forest destruction goes beyond the extinction of species. It also includes the loss of fertile topsoil. In the mid-1980s the Bureau of Soil in the Philippines estimated that the equivalent of 100,000 hectares of soil, one metre thick, was lost each year in the Philippines. This dramatically reduces the prospect for sustainable agriculture in the future in a country where the human population is continuing to increase.

On a global scale levels of soil erosion is extremely worrying. Professor David Pimentel and his team of researchers at Cornell University in the US estimate that, world-wide, 75 billion tonnes of topsoil are lost every year. The greatest losses, averaging between 30 to 40 tonnes per hectare per crop, are in Africa, Asia and Latin America. Even in the US the figure is around 17 tonnes per hectare.[17]

When the soil is stripped from the land during heavy monsoons it is swept away before raging floods into the rivers, lakes and coastal lagoons. There the mud silts up rivers and kills the delicate coral reefs. The final result is a dramatic fall in fish stocks and a consequent drop in protein for the poor fishing communities. The removal of the forest cover also leaves an imprint on local climatic conditions. In recent years long periods of drought have been much more common than they were in the past.

What's on offer to address the crisis?

Given the pain that the debt crisis has caused to poor people and the toll it has taken on the global environment one would expect that the crisis would be addressed as a matter of urgency. Unfortunately, this is not happening.

In 1996 the World Bank in the face of opposition from the IMF, and footdragging by the Paris Club,[18] put together a debt relief initiative for highly indebted poor countries (HIPC). HIPC comes after a long line of commercial debt initiatives, like the Baker Plan of 1985, the Brady plan of 1989 and the Trinidad/ Naples terms proposed by the former British Prime Minister John Major. All of these failed to tackle the debt problem in an effective or comprehensive way. They generally favoured the interests of the creditors. Under the Baker plan, for example, debtor countries by implementing reforms were expected to grow themselves out of debt. Debt-for-equity and other privatization initiatives were also promoted. The Brady plan included issuing bonds and trade related actions.

HIPC aims at involving all the creditors, banks and governments and for the first time will deal with debts owed to multilateral institutions like the World Bank and IMF. It is estimated that only forty-one of the world's poorest countries would be eligible for significant debt relief under this initiative. Nicaragua would not be due to receive much help until 2002 and the Honduran debts are not large enough to make it eligible for relief.[19]

Initially, some aspects of HIPC was welcomed by campaigning groups. According to its designers, the aim of HIPC is to reduce debt to a level which countries can afford without endangering economic development or increasing human impoverishment. In other words, debt servicing should not undermine sustainability.

But what constitutes sustainability? To pay its debts countries need to earn foreign exchange through selling goods and services on the export market. HIPC deems that a country's debt-servicing management is sustainable if it does not exceed 25 per cent of export earnings. Campaigning groups feel that other economic and social criteria should also be applied, given the particular needs of individual countries. For example, account should be taken of the percentage of the national budget which is spent on debt servicing. As we have seen in discussing the cases of Bolivia and Zambia much more of the country's budget is spent on debt servicing than on health, education, social services and ecological programmes combined. This can hardly promote balanced and sustainable development. The British-based group CAFOD argues that 'without poverty at the centre of assessment of debt sustainability the HIPC exercise is unlikely to achieve levels of debt relief sufficient for equitable economic growth and ultimately poverty reduction'.[19]

Another major criticism is that eligible countries have to undergo what amounts to six years of both World Bank structural adjustment programmes and IMF's Enhanced Structural Adjustment Facility (ESAF). This is totally unrealistic: to date very few countries have remained on the austerity track for more than a year or two. These conditions would mean that very few countries would benefit from the HIPC initiative until well into the next millennium. The only country to benefit thus far is Uganda.

It is totally unacceptable to expect poor, debtor countries to wait for six years for significant debt relief. Given the pressures on the governments of poor countries very few have been able to sustain an austerity programme for more than a year or so. If compliance with a ESAF programme is a *sine qua non* for benefiting from HIPC then very few countries will be able to avail of the debt relief until well into the next millennium. Little wonder that a long-time debt campaigner like Jo Marie

Griesgraber of the Center of Concern in Washington considers that 'HIPC is designed with the creditors in mind: it is slow and complicated and costs them as little as possible while requiring maximum conformity to the creditors' interpretation of responsible economic reform i.e., structural adjustment'.[20]

Opposition to HIPC has come, not just from Third World countries and campaigning organisations, but from mainline politicians. In an article which appeared in the London *Times* 'Time to Stop the Third World Debt Treadmill' in the week before the 1997 IMF and World Bank meeting in Hong Kong, the former Prime Minister, Lord Callaghan, criticised the present World Bank and IMF strategy for addressing Third World Debt. According to Callaghan, the IMF's and World Bank's proposals aimed at reducing the debt burden for the Highly Indebted Poor Countries (HIPC) does not go far enough. The relief is too slow, the conditions are too strict and the number of countries that will benefit is too few. Only debts incurred before a designated 'cut-off' date are eligible for bilateral reduction under HIPC. For many countries that date is located in the early or mid-1980s. Debt campaigners are demanding that the cut-off point be pushed back into the mid-1990s.

Much the same criticism was directed against HIPC in Britain by the influential International Development Committee. The MPs recommended that the HIPC process be speeded up considerably. The time scale for checking a country's track record should be reduced to three years. The criteria for deciding whether a given country can sustain a debt-relief programme should be relaxed. The criteria should also include domestic debt. This would then mean that spending on health, education and welfare would be taken into account. Finally, they criticised the secrecy that surrounds the IMF/World Bank *modus operandi*. They called for much more transparency in the way these institutions operate.

Another criticism of HIPC is that it does not include countries like Jamaica, the Philippines or Brazil. In the categories drawn up by the World Bank and the IMF these are not severely-indebted-low-income countries; rather they are classed as middle-income countries and therefore do not qualify for HIPC type relief. Yet the poor in these countries live in appalling, inhuman circumstances where people and whole communities lack sanitation, access to clean, drinkable water and sufficient food to meet daily calorie requirements.

In Jamaica almost a quarter of the population live below the poverty line on $2 or less per day. There is only one doctor for over 7,000 people. But, given the widespread poverty, most people cannot afford a doctor when they are sick. In Jamaica in recent years there has been an increase in the number of those affected by HIV and AIDS. Yet the government can do little to help the sick when the 1997 budget allotted five times more for debt servicing than for health care and ten times more than for education.

Jubilee 2000

Jubilee 2000 is campaigning for a once-off cancellation of the back-log of unpayable debts to mark the millennium. The Jubilee campaign began in Britain and by mid-1998 there were Jubilee campaigns in most European countries, the US and Canada and, most promising of all, a Jubilee campaign for Africa. Twenty seven countries kicked off with a meeting in Accra, Ghana in April 1998.

Jubilee 2000 is campaigning for debt relief for poor countries, both severely-indebted low-income and middle-income countries. Low-income countries with an annual income per person of less then $700 should receive full remission of unpayable debts. Countries with an annual income per person of between $700 and $2,000 should receive substantial debt remission.

Jubilee 2000 knows that the initiative it is proposing will not solve all the problems besetting Third World countries. It is, however, meant to give a clear signal to the poor of the world that others care and wish to see them breaking the shackles of poverty that cause misery to hundreds of millions of people.

The jubilee initiative draws its inspiration from the Judeo-Christian tradition. As is clear from Leviticus 25, the Year of Jubilee was seen as a way to re-establish a just social order at regular moments in Israel's history. The Jubilee was an extension of the Sabbath. It called for release for Israelites who had become enslaved through economic misfortune (Lev 25:35-38); restoration of land to the original owner (Lev 25:23-28), and forgiveness of debts: 'At the end of every seven years you must grant a remission. Now the nature of the remission is this; every creditor who holds the person of his neighbour in bond must grant him remission; he may not exact payment from his fellow or his brother once the latter appeals to Yahweh.' (Deut 15:1-2)

Israel was a community shaped by its belief that their God, Yahweh had rescued them from slavery in Egypt and had obliged them to develop genuine bonds of mutual support within their community life. There could be no genuine community if a small proportion of the population owned most of the land and wealth and exploited the poor, starving masses at every opportunity. The cry in Deuteronomy 15:5 – 'let there be no poor among you' – arises from a spirit of gratitude to Yahweh for his gifts, especially the gift of freedom and the land.

Because Israel had experienced Yahweh's compassion it is understandable that the laws governing lending would be sensitive to the plight of debtors. Exodus 22:25 warns creditors that they must not impoverish the poor and worsen their plight. Charging interest was seen as way of impaling the poor on the treadmill of debt that might deprive them of the necessities of life.

Deuteronomy 24 goes even further and forbids a creditor from acting in a high handed or haughty way towards a debtor by entering the debtor's house to recover a pledge. The creditor is expected to wait outside the house until the debtor carries out the pledge himself. In the biblical perspective, if the creditor entered the house of the debtor without permission it would be seen as an insult to the dignity of the debtors.

The same chapter also forbids (Deut 24:26) confiscating the means of livelihood of a person as collateral on a debt. This was very understandable in an agricultural society where most people lived from hand to mouth. Where a creditor takes a mill stone as a pledge, it would literally deprive the debtor and his family of basic life-supporting instrument. This was considered intolerable.

The millennium celebrates the two-thousandth anniversary of the birth of Jesus. The harsh socio-economic realities that obtained in Roman-occupied Palestine at the time of Jesus was marked by indebtedness, heavy taxes, widespread begging, and slavery. Poor country people had to hire out their labour just to stay alive. This was the context of Jesus's preaching. His message was meant to be good news for the poor. It is also worth noting that the second petition in the Lord's Prayer in Matthew's Gospel asks God to forgive us our debts, as we have forgiven those who are in debt to us (Mt 6:12). Jesus was well aware that cancelling debts freed poor people from a culture and economics of dependency and gave people real freedom of choice.

Luke's Gospel, which was addressed to a gentile audience in the period after the destruction of Jerusalem, highlights the issue of debt and jubilee. The congregation was composed of both rich and poor people. Luke's message was one of challenge to the rich to share with the poor, and one effective way to do this was to forgive debts. To refuse to recognize the needs of the poor and respond to them evoked strong condemnation from Luke. 'But alas for you who are rich; you are having your consolation now' (Lk 6:24).

Proclaiming the jubilee with its accompanying debt relief instruction is central to the message of Jesus as found in Luke's Gospel. Jesus presents the focus of his mission in a dramatic way by reading from Book of Isaiah at the synagogue in Nazareth:

> The spirit of the Lord has been given to me,
> for he has anointed me.
> He has sent me to bring the good news to the poor,
> to proclaim liberty to captives
> to the blind new sight,
> to set the downtrodden free,
> to proclaim the Lord's year of favour

In Luke's Gospel, though the petition in the Lord's Prayer speaks of forgiving sins in return for us forgiving debts (Lk 11:3b-4a), one could argue that debt relief was on Luke's mind. Later on in his gospel there is approval for the shrewd steward who writes off debts even though his motives were far from pure (Lk 16:1-8).

Given the prominence of debt cancellation in the Hebrew and Christian Scriptures debt write-offs for the poor should be at the top of the Churches' agenda. The parallel between what is happening in the Third World today and what was happening at the time when Deuteronomy and Leviticus were written and at the time when Jesus was preaching are very striking. In all cases the debt treadmill is seen as responsible for consigning huge segments of the population to perpetual, life-destroying poverty.

The literature of the early Church, especially from the fourth and fifth centuries, is fully of denunciations of those who prey on the poor through demanding usurious interest on loans. Though much of the teaching was directed against clerics who charged interest, the twelfth canon of the First Council of Carthage (345) and the thirty-sixth canon of the Council of Aix (789) declared it to be reprehensible even for laymen to make money by lending at interest.

Condemnation of usury continued into the Middle Ages. The Third Council of Lateran (1179) and the Second Council of Lyons (1274) condemned usurers. The Council of Vienne (1311) went as far as to declare that anyone who obstinately maintained that there was no sin in the practice of demanding interest should be punished as a heretic.

The teaching on usury in the Christian Churches began to change in the wake of the Reformation in the sixteenth century. While Luther, Melanchthon and Zwingli condemned taking interest on a loan, Calvin permitted it, especially if the loan was made to rich people. Gradually, even in the Catholic tradition interest on a loan became morally acceptable as long as it was not considered excessive. Once it came to be accepted that money was a productive commodity it seemed logical to charge interest. The interest was meant to compensate the lender for the risk of losing the capital or for the loss of those profits a person would experience if he/she had not made the loan in the first place. The tradition also distinguished between a loan for consumption and a loan for production. The Church accepted that taking money on a loan for production was just and proper.

While it must be acknowledged that the Scriptures seem to prohibit taking interest on any loan, especially when one to a fellow Israelite, modern Catholic moral teaching does not consider it unjust to oblige a person to pay interest on a debt. Pope John Paul II, in his encyclical *Centesimus Annus*, acknowledges that the 'principle that debts must be paid is certainly just' (n. 35).

There is, however, continuity between the biblical and patristic teaching and contemporary Christian and Catholic social teaching. All are agreed that the rights and needs of people must take precedent over the rights of property or capital. If repaying debts becomes so burdensome and destructive that the human well-being of vast numbers of people is endangered then debt servicing is clearly immoral in the Christian tradition.

This stems for an insistence, found in Scripture and in the Christian tradition, that property or capital do not have absolute rights. There is no support for the absolute character of the claim found in the Code of Justinian (529 A.D.) that owners enjoyed *jus utendi, jus fruendi* and *jus abutendi* of their capital, land or private property. In Roman law the owner had an almost absolute right to use property in any way he saw fit.

The Bible had a very different vision of reality. The rights of the poor, the orphan, the widow, the stranger takes precedent over property rights. As a consequence the rights inherent in debt obligations give way in the face of the over-riding right of people to food, clothing, shelter, health-care and education. The moral imperative to promote the well-being of others, especially the vulnerable, takes precedent over the obligation to pay debts.

Many of the measures taken by the multilateral agencies like the World Bank and the IMF give priority to debt contracts, rather than the well-being of people. A typical SAPs programme that includes currency devaluation, trade liberalization, cut-backs in health, education and welfare and retrenchment in the public service regularly gives priority to the rights of lenders even when these actions impoverish vast numbers of people.

Because of these similarities between the impact of debt on poor as seen in the scriptures and the impact on the poor in our world today one would expect that Christian leaders would condemn the evils perpetrated on the poor through Third World debt payments. Calls for debt cancellation have come from the World Council of Churches, the Vatican, and a number of episcopal conferences. In the encyclical letter, *Tertio Millennio Adveniente*, written to help Christians prepare for the millennium, Pope John Paul II urged believers 'to raise their voice on behalf of the poor of the world, proposing the Jubilee as an appropriate time to give thought, among other things, to reducing substantially, if not cancelling outright, the international debt which seriously threatens the future of many nations' (n. 51). Similar calls for debt cancellation came from the Lambeth Conference in July 1998 where the assembled bishops recommended that each Province of the Anglican Communion should support the Jubilee 2000 campaign and that each diocese should give 0.7 percent of its income in solidarity with the Jubilee movement.

In his World Day of Peace message for 1999 Pope John Paul II called for a 'sincere effort to find a solution to the frightening problem of the international debt of the poorest nations.' And he went on: 'International financial institutions have initiated concrete steps in this regard which merit appreciation. I appeal to all those involved in this problem, especially the more affluent nations, to provide the support necessary to ensure the full success of this initiative. An immediate and vigorous effort is needed, as we look to the year 2000, to ensure that the greatest possible number of nations will be able to extricate themselves from a now intolerable situation'.

In February 1999 a statement from the Irish Catholic Bishops' Conference entitled *Put Life Before Debt* stated: 'This debt burden remains one of the most significant obstacles to social and economic progress in some of the poorest countries in the world, particularly in Sub-Saharan Africa. A billion people in these countries are enslaved by foreign debts incurred in many cases over 20 years ago with the strong encouragement of Western financial institutions. Moreover, it is these poorest people, particularly women and children, who suffer most from the effects of this debt burden. They are deprived of the basic services that most of us take for granted in Ireland; primary education, health care, clean water, adequate food and shelter. Where debt can only be repaid by denying such services then they should be deemed unpayable'.

Despite support from the leadership of the Churches few people, including well-informed Christians, would consider that action on debt forgiveness has been high on the agenda of the various Churches, especially, in the First World. The Jubilee 2000 campaign offers Christians an opportunity to lend their voice in support of freeing the poor of the world from modern day enslavement. The statement by the Irish Catholic Bishops came out in fully support for the Jubilee 2000 Campaign.

Jubilee 2000 groups have sprung up in many countries in the North and South. 70,000 people took to the streets of Birmingham for the G8 meeting on May 12, 1998. They formed a human chain around the area where the leaders of the G8 were meeting. The symbolism of the action was captured in the caption 'Break the Chain of Debt'.

Though the leaders of the G8 did not come up with any new initiative on debt at the Birmingham meeting they certainly knew that a lot of people from Britain and overseas were thoroughly disgusted with the lack of progress on debt. The British Prime Minister, Tony Blair, aware that an articulate constituency was lobbying for change, felt it necessary to leave his G8 colleagues at a country mansion outside Birmingham and return to the city to meet the protesters.

The director of Jubilee 2000 UK, Ann Pettifor, was critical of the lack of satisfactory debt relief measures at the Birmingham

Summit: 'This is a huge disappointment for the 70,000 people who joined the human chain in Birmingham and the hundreds of millions around the world who suffer under the burden of unpayable debt'.[21] Nevertheless she did feel that the Birmingham demonstration had achieved a lot: 'Three months ago debt wasn't even on the agenda of the G8 Summit. But now it will be remembered as the Debt Summit. For the first time the world's most powerful leaders met the people's voice head on'.[22]

After Birmingham, Jubilee 2000 continued to intensify its campaign. At the G7 meeting in Cologne in June 1999 the leaders of the seven riches countries on the planet promised a $70 billion relief package. At first glance this sounds very generous and impressive. However on closer analysis it is totally inadequate. $70 billion is less than half the $217 billion debt mountain that is crushing the poorest countries in the world.

The bulk of the $70 billion package is not new money at all. $25 billion had already been committed at the G7 meeting in Birmingham the previous year. A further $20 billion is composed of country to country loans that were not being paid off anyway. Cancelling these is merely a book-keeping exercise. This means that the real sum is a mere $25 billion, but even this is written in terms of future payments. So in fact the total package boils down, in 1999, figures to something between $12 and $14 billion dollars. This is destined to be shared among 36 of the poorest countries on earth and so, in fact, it is a paltry amount. The bottom line is that the money which poor countries ought to be using to educate its people and provide basic health care facilities will still be used mainly to service the country's debts. Finally the Cologne initiative contains no reference to an independent mediation mechanism where creditors and debtors alike would negotiate the terms and conditions which should prevail in the debt relief negotiations. Debt relief is still tightly linked to structural adjustment and ESAF (the IMF Enchanced Structural Adjustment Facility), which has been widely criticised by NGOs for exacerbating poverty in many countries.

On September 21st 1999 the Jubilee 2000 campaigners and celebrities like the U2 singer Bono met with Pope John Paul II. During the meeting the Pope agreed to ask world leaders to cancel the $217 billion as part of the millennium celebrations.

This lobbying did have some immediate effect. During the IMF/World Bank meeting at the end of September 1999 a further $26 was added to the debt relief fund for HIPC countries. In his speech to the meeting President Clinton offered for the first time to write off 100% of loans from the poorest countries. He has urged the US Congress to allocate $970 million to speed up debt relief.[23] The NGO community while gratified that forgiving Third World Debt has taken on a momentum in the lead up the millennium is not convinced that Congress will respond to the President's request and are still worried that the conditions laid down the IMF are still too stringent.

Other elements of Catholic Social Teaching which would relieve the debt burden and promote global equity
It is important to remember that even a once-off cancellation would leave in place many of the unjust structures that caused the debt crisis in the first instance. To prevent this from happening policy initiatives like the following should be put in place as a matter of urgency.

1. Lift the burden of debt from the shoulder of those people who were least responsible for contracting it in the first instance. It is important to include in debt cancellation initiatives countries like the Philippines and Brazil which are classified as severely-indebted, middle-income countries. While these countries have a minority of rich people and a sizable middle class the majority of their population live below the poverty line.

Properly managed debt relief could be used as an instrument to stimulate much needed development for the poor. The scheme would envisage the debtor redeeming a small part of the external debt in local currency and making those funds available to non-government organisations involved in welfare, health care, and environmental activities.

2. The debt burden should be shared equitably among all those responsible for causing the debt. This would include creditor institutions, debtor governments, the multilateral financial institutions (IMF/World Bank), Northern corporations and the elite in Third World countries who incurred the debt in the first instance. A complete write-off of the IMF's exposure to Africa would require a mere 10 per cent of its $36 billion gold reserve. The IMF could well afford such a venture. To date the Brady and Baker plans and similar initiatives placed the burden of payment and adjustment almost exclusively on the debtor nations, despite the fact that the lending policies of private banks and capital flight contributed greatly to the current situation. In addition governments and creditor institutions knew that much of the original borrowing was undertaken by illegally constituted regimes often violation of the laws of lending countries.

3. Many of the debts that were incurred do not meet the requirements necessary for a just contract. For this reason it would be very worthwhile if an alliance of debtor countries challenged the legality of 'odious' debts in some international forum, possibly the International Court of Justice at the Hague. After the US ended the Spanish domination of Cuba in the wake of the Spanish American war in 1898, the Spanish government argued that the US should assume Cuba's debts. The US refused to do so, arguing that the debts were incurred by the Government of Spain for its own purposes and through its own agents in whose creation the people of Cuba had no voice.

The same principle was applied when Britain challenged Costa Rica's attempt to cancel the debt of its former dictator to the Royal Bank of Canada. US Supreme Court Justice, William Howard Taft who was the arbitrator in the case dismissed the claim. He held that because the bank had lent the money for no legitimate use the claim was illegitimate. A similar logic surely extends to much of the Third World debt today. The people of the Philippines had no involvement in the debts incurred by the Marcos regime. Likewise the people of Uganda had little involvement in the debts of the brutal dictator Idi Amin and yet they are now saddled with paying them even though it is undermining their basic right to a decent way of life.

4. Some mechanism should be found whereby poor countries could file for bankruptcy. The majority of these countries have much smaller economies than have trans-national corporations. Yet these institutions can file for bankruptcy if they get into financial difficulties. It should be possible for some of the global financial institutions like the World Bank and legal institutions like the World Court at the Hague to devise a nation-state version of US chapter 11 legislation. This legislation protects a debtor company from creditors until such time as it can reorganise itself and be in a position to repay its debtors. Chapter 9 of that legislation also regulates the insolvency of municipalities. Municipalities are not expected either to run down their social and educational services or tax their citizens excessively in order to pay its creditors .

The arbitration institutions that might address questions of insolvency would be tasked with assessing both the nature of the debts and the economic capacity of a country to pay its debts. Consideration would need to be given to the ability of the debtor country to meet the fundamental needs of its citizens to have adequate food, clothing, shelter, basic education, healthcare and environmental protection. Fair and equitable procedures would ensure that both the debtors and the creditors are justly treated. This can best be achieved if both the debtors and creditors are allowed to nominate people on to the appropriate arbitration panel and the whole process is open and transparent. It would be helpful if such international debt arbitration panels were recognised in international law.

5. Address factors that add to the burden of debt for development countries. These include currency fluctuations, declining aid budgets, unilateral increases in interest rates and protectionist trade policies.

6. Support Third World country's efforts to foster economic self-reliance and sustainable development. Programmes that promote redistribution of wealth, ecological sustainability and participation of people in their own development are the most effective ways of raising living standards.

7. There is also a need for a debt monitoring agency in countries presently plagued by debt and who are still borrowing money. The purpose of the agency would be to raise questions about the advisability of new loans and to monitor how these loans are spent. The need for an independent, competent and well-resourced agency is clear when one remembers that much of the borrowing by corrupt, dictatorial regimes in the 1970s took place in secret with little or no consideration of how these loans might promote the common good. In many situations the loans actually intensified rather than relieved poverty.

To avoid a repeat of such blunders, the members of the debt management agency ought to be drawn from a wide segment of the community. State sector representatives might be drawn from the Central Bank and Department of Finance. The commercial sector might be represented by people from commercial or financial institutions. Representatives from NGOs and the Churches and other religions should also have their place in such an agency. Deliberations of the debt management agency should be made public so as to promote discussion about development policies and lending initiatives in the wider society. In the 1970s many decisions were made by young economic apparatchiks who had little knowledge of the development needs of poor people and communities.

8. Finally, promote a more just international economic system. Reforms are urgently needed to provide more democratic representation and decision-making in international economic institutions like the World Bank and especially, the International Monetary Fund. These institutions have routinely misjudged the global economic situation in their desire to promote economic globalisation. Just before the Asian collapse in 1997 a World Bank report lauded the economic performance of Korea, Thailand and Malaysia.

In the wake of the Asian financial collapse, right-wing economists like Milton Friedman criticised the IMF for its interventionist approach. According to him, this hindered the normal shake-up which the so-called 'invisible hand' of the free-market would bring about. Other economists like Geffrey Sachs of Harvard University also blamed the IMF for exacerbating the situation in Asia: 'Instead of dousing the fire, the IMF in effect screamed fire in the theatre'.[24] Sachs claims that the IMF-imposed austerity programme will force these countries into a severe recession which will be in nobody's interest. There are those, of course, who claim that the IMF's role in the Asian crisis was dictated by the US Treasury and that it will only benefit Northern, mainly US financial institutions and corporations.

The United Nations Conference on Trade and Development (UNCTAD) in its *Trade and Development Report 1998* makes the same point. It contends that the IMF's advice to raise interest rates made things worse.

Rather than ease the burden of refinancing on domestic firms by granting additional credit, the recommended policy response was to raise interest rates. This depressed asset prices further and increased balance sheet losses of firms and their need to repay or hedge their foreign indebtedness quickly by liquidating assets and selling the domestic currency.[25]

As a result, foreign investors' interests were, in general protected. The report goes on to claim that foreign lenders 'unlike domestic lenders, emerged from the crisis without substantial loss, even though they had accepted exposure to risk just as other lenders had done'.

Calls for reform at the IMF are coming from the Right and the Left. Unfortunately, it appears that it is the affluent North rather than the impoverished South that will benefit from increasing the pace of globalisation, through pursuing its neo-liberal economic model. Its macro-economic policies focus almost exclusively on tackling inflation and curbing budget deficits. Everything else – jobs, poverty alleviation and environmental sustainability – is edited out of the equation or put on the long finger. In Asia massive currency devaluations have made Korean and Thai assets very cheap for US corporations. Increasing the mobility of global capital will make it possible for Northern companies to buy into viable companies at bargain basement prices.

What the South needs is greater accountability in the financial system, protection from currency speculators, more participation in their own development initiatives, stable and fair prices for goods, access to markets in the North and greater aid and support for alternative development initiatives. More democratic voting arrangements and less secrecy would enhance the efficiency and credibility of multilateral lending institutions. These institutions might also give a lead in controlling the movement of speculative capital around the world. Thirty years ago 90 per cent of foreign exchange transactions related to trade and long-term investment and 5 per cent to speculation. With the liberalisation of capital markets today 95 per cent of transactions are speculative and only 5 per cent pertain to real trade or investment. In 1972 the Nobel Prize winner economist, James Tobin proposed a tax on speculative financial transactions. Such a tax pegged at the very low rate of 0.1 per cent would at present earn $100 billion dollars a year.[26] Such money could be used for debt relief and development projects.

It is also true that the credibility and efficiency of multilateral lending agencies would be enhanced by more democratic voting arrangements and less secrecy. Without major structural changes in the international financial institutions, the stranglehold that the economically powerful nations (G7) have on them will continue. They will simply continue to develop policies that promote the interests of their paymasters.

Given the terrible pain and havoc which Third World debt has wreaked, the Christian Churches should use the millennium celebration to campaign for debt forgiveness and for a more just, international economic order, based on co-operation and sharing, rather than predatory economic policies. It would bring genuine liberation and well-being to the poor and would be good news for Earth itself and all future generations.

CHAPTER THREE

Global Warming:
a Challenge to Christians

Few people, either in the rich North or the poor South, worry about the phenomenon called global warming. For the vast majority of families the usual day-to-day problems top their list of priorities. These include coping with a rise in the cost of living, an increase in rent or mortgage payments, the cost of health-care or education, access to a job or adequate welfare payments and pension provisions. Yet global warming is a serious problem. Even today it impinges on the lives of millions of people through the increased frequency and ferocity of storms like hurricane Mitch which devastated Central America in November 1998. More ominously, experts predict that, unless radical remedial action is taken now, the effects of global warming will devastate the lives of hundreds of millions of people in the next century.

This is the dilemma that surrounds many environmental issues: though, in the abstract, many would agree that they are very serious in themselves, they do not seem to impact directly on the lives of ordinary people. Consequently it is difficult to mobilise the ordinary citizen and public officials to take remedial action, especially if it would make them feel the pinch in their personal lives.

Global warming is normal
It is important to remember that global warming is essential for life on earth. If the earth was like the moon and lacked an atmosphere no life could exist on the planet. The average temperature would be around -18 degrees Celsius. It is because the earth has a protective atmospheric mantle that the average temperature of our planet is around 15 degrees Celsius. In order

to explain global warming the atmosphere is often compared to the glass in a greenhouse. Like the glass in the greenhouse the atmosphere allows solar radiation to pass through and heat the surface of the earth. Most of the solar radiation is absorbed by the earth's surface. However, some of the long-wave radiation that is reflected back off the surface of the earth is, in turn, absorbed by the atmosphere and reflected back to earth. This is a natural global process, which regulates climate conditions and maintains the warmth and moisture essential for life on earth. As long as both the percentages of the various gases in atmosphere and solar radiation remains constant an equilibrium is established and life can adapt to that regime in the different habitats of the world.

Human intervention introduces instability

Problems arise, however, when the composition of gases in the atmosphere changes. This is precisely what has happened especially in recent decades. Human activity, mainly associated with the burning of fossil fuel, has changed the chemistry of the atmosphere. As the volume of what are called greenhouse gases like Carbon Dioxide (CO_2), Carbon Monoxide (CO), Methane, Nitrogen Oxides (Nox), including Nitrogen Dioxide (NO_2) and Chloroflurocarbons (CFCs) increases the temperature close to the earth's surface rise gradually.

Scientists working with the Intergovernmental Panel on Climate Change (IPCC) have estimated that the levels of carbon dioxide, one of the most important greenhouse gases, has increased by 25 per cent since the beginning of the Industrial Revolution. This gas is produced primarily when fossil fuels are burned to provide energy for our expanding industrial society. Whether it is directly related to the increase in greenhouse gases or not, the climate records show that nine of the ten hottest years since records began have occurred since 1983 and five of those years happened in the 1990s.[1]

If present trends continue the IPCC scientists expect a further 30 per cent increase in the levels of carbon in the air over the next fifty years. It is predicted that such an increase in carbon dioxide and other greenhouse gases could lead to an average temperature rise of between 1.5 and 4.5 degrees Celsius by the year 2030. Some might think that such a small increase is insignificant. Not so: during the last Ice Age the average global temperature was only five degrees Celsius colder than it is today, and yet much of Ireland and Northern Europe was covered by ice.

Consequences

What are the likely consequences of global warming? An average global temperature increase of 3 per cent could lead to an increase of more than 10 degrees Celsius in both the Arctic and Antarctic. This would melt much of the ice-sheet and lead to a 20 to 50 centimetre rise in the level of the ocean by the year 2050. In 1998 the Larsen B ice shelf in the Antarctic, which covers an area of 7,500 miles, broke off and began to melt.

The melting of the ice sheets in both polar regions will speed up the warming process through what is known as the albedo effect. This means that light coloured regions of the planet, like the polar regions, have high albedo and reflect more of the sun's rays back into space. Darker regions, on the other hand, absorb more heat and consequently increase the overall warming effect.

A rise in sea levels will have a devastating impact on people in many Pacific islands, low-lying areas like Bangladesh, the Nile or Mekong deltas. It is estimated that it will lead to the permanent displacement of tens of millions of people. The effect of the rise in the level of the ocean is, even at this moment, being felt in Europe. British scientists claim that global warming caused a massive chunk of Beachy Head in East Sussex in Britain to collapse into the sea in January 1999. Mr Ray Kent a spokesman for the Environment Agency stated that 'it is basically down to climate change. The level of the sea is rising, so bigger waves are hitting against the cliff base, causing bigger vibrations to reverberate up the cliff'.[2] Dr John Sweeney of St Patrick's College, Maynooth believes that global warming will bring increase flooding into the Sandymount area of Dublin (*The Irish Times*, 2 December 1997).

Global warming will also mean much more erratic weather conditions. One of the world's largest insurance companies, Munich Re, issued a report in 1990 on the impact of global warming on the insurance business. The report stated that 'if water temperatures increase by 0.5 to 1 degree C in the course of the next few decades, we can expect an extension of the hurricane season by several weeks and a considerable increase in the frequency and intensity of hurricanes'.[3] This will have very serious consequences for insurance policies in many parts of the world. It would seem that such predictions are being borne out. Experts estimated that Mitch was the worst storm to strike Central America in two hundred years.

Scientists also predict that rainfall patterns will change dramatically. This may have a knock-on effect on food production. Some major croplands in the temperate zones, like the prairie lands of North America, will, most likely, be lost to agriculture because of drought. There is also the likelihood that desertification will increase in many sub-tropical areas.

The disruptive impact on agriculture will in turn have a huge impact on the lives of ordinary people, especially those in the Third World. According to Dr Sweeney, global warming will mean wetter winters and drier summers in Ireland. It is too early to say yet whether the hurricane winds that lashed Ireland during the Christmas period in 1997 and 1998 can be attributed to global warming. Dr Mark Maslin of the Environmental Change Research Centre at the University of London argues that rapid warming 'increases global storminess' (*The Guardian*, 7 October 1998, p. 5).

Climate change will also put stress on many fragile ecosystems like forests and grasslands. Because of the suddenness of the change many habitats will not be easily able to adapt to the new climatic conditions. If this happens many species will be forced over the precipice of extinction. Migratory birds, for example, may find that the salt marshes and mudflats on which they depend for food will disappear even with a relative small rise in the levels of the ocean.

Countries of the North are mainly responsible

In the face of problems like global warming, there is often a tendency to lay the blame evenly across the peoples of the world. The truth is that the peoples of the Northern industrialised countries are mainly responsible for global warming. Unfortunately in the words of the Second World Climate Conference, 'in many cases the impact will be felt most severely in regions already under stress, mainly in the developing countries'.[4]

In the early 1990s the industrialised nations, which comprise only about 20 per cent of the world's population, were responsible for between 75 and 80 per cent of all greenhouse gases. A chart on page 11 of the World Council of Churches' (WCC) study on global warming entitled *Accelerated Climate Change: Sign of Peril, Test of Faith* estimates that in the period between 1800 and 1988 the most developed countries – the US, Europe, Japan and Australia – were responsible for 83.7 per cent of the increase in CO_2 in the atmosphere. The contribution of the least developed countries, including India and China, amounted to only 16.3 per cent. The WCC document states clearly that 'global warming brings into sharp focus the inequality of economic relationships between the North and the South'.[5]

Action is needed now

Global warming will continue to plague the peoples of the earth unless Northern countries drastically reduce their consumption of fossil fuel. Is this possible? Professor Ernst U. von Weizsacher of the Wuppertal Institute for Climate, Environment and Energy in Germany, believes it is. He argues that countries in the North could cut their use of fossil fuel dramatically without causing too much hardship to the majority of their people. In his opinion there are still enormous possibilities for energy-saving strategies. Some of these involve improved technology, others require social, political and economic changes. Energy-saving heaters and cookers could become 100 per cent more energy-efficient. More efficient insulation in dwellings could reduce domestic heating consumption by almost 90 per cent. Good public transport, bicycle lanes and improved car engine efficiency could reduce the consumption of petrol and oil considerably. Alternative energy sources like wind, wave, and photovoltaic could reduce our reliance on fossil fuel considerably. The technology to accomplish all of these initiatives already exists. The Dutch Government estimates that they could cut the CO_2 emissions by 80 per cent during the next fifty years without stunting the growth of their economy.

A 'Carbon Tax' is needed

One way to change attitudes and speed up the introduction of more efficient technology is to introduce 'green taxes'. According to von Weizacker, a green tax on fossil fuel tax could help reflect the real cost of using these resources. The price tag should reflect the real cost of extracting oil or coal with all the negative consequences of such activity. It should also take account of the harmful impact of fossil fuel extraction and consumption on human health and the environment, especially regarding global warming. Those who favour this approach also point out that an energy tax would help stimulate new inventions that would lead to greater levels of energy efficiency.

Some people might groan at the thought of another tax on the shoulders of people who feel that they are already over-taxed with income tax, value-add tax and a variety of local taxes. For this reason von Weizacker recommends that green taxes should be introduced gradually and that they should be revenue-neutral. This simply means that the revenue collected from fossil fuel energy products would be offset by major reductions in income tax and sale taxes. It would also be essential to protect the living standard of poor people in First World countries who are often more dependent on fossil fuel sources for their heating and transport needs than are their middle class neighbours. In order to avoid eroding further their standard of living it may be necessary to introduce compensatory social welfare payments to off-set the increase in energy costs.

Overall, most economists agree that a 'carbon tax' makes good economic sense because it will help promote energy efficiency and lead to the phasing out of dirty, polluting industries. It would also create more jobs. The Council on Economic Priorities in the US estimate that investment in energy-efficient technologies produces four times more jobs than a similar level of investment in a new power stations.[6] A study by the Economic and Social Research Institute (ESRI) of Ireland in May 1997 recommended that a European Union wide 'greenhouse gas tax' should be levied on all polluters in the industrial, agricultural and transport sector.[7] They felt that this would be a more effective way of curbing greenhouse emissions and protecting the environment than relying on regulations alone. Professor John FitzGerald of the ESRI was very critical of the Irish government's very dilatory stance on the carbon tax.

A carbon tax would have a major and beneficial impact on food production. There has been a huge increase in the use of fossil fuel in agriculture since World War II. This can be seen both in the increased use of mechanical energy on the farm and also in the use of petrochemical fertilisers and pesticides. Apart from contributing to global warming and decreasing the fertility of the soils, petrochemical-driven agriculture has favoured large agribusiness corporations at the expense of family farm units. Large companies have easy access to cheap credit, heavy machinery, chemical pesticides, fertiliser, automated processing units, and their transport costs are low. While the food produced in such a way might be cheap, the human, animal welfare and environmental costs are very high. These include the loss of topsoil, the increased toxicity of soils and water sources, the loss of biodiversity, extremely cruel conditions for animals, poor quality food and rural decline and depopulation.

A substantial tax on energy could help turn all that around. It would make it more cost-effective to produce food locally, using organic methods which in turn would favour family farm units. The knock-on effect would be seen in the availability of fresh, more nutritious food. It would mean that less energy would be used in processing and transporting food. Less intensive cultivation would mean more fertile soils, a greater diversity of crops, and revitalised rural communities with more people finding jobs in agriculture. In October 1997 five senior scientific advisers on climate change to the UK Government warned that inaction on global warming could mean that 'millions of people will become environmental refugees and starve because politicians are failing to prepare for inevitable climate change resulting from man's activities'.[8]

In order to minimise the negative aspect of 'green' taxes it is important that they be introduced gradually. Von Weizsacker recommends that a 5 per cent annual increase in the price of fossil fuel or nuclear-derived energy would gradually shift the balance in energy costs away from fossil fuels towards the more benign forms of renewable energy. These include hydropower, solar, wind, wave and biomass derived energy. A gradual, well-planned, introduction of these more benign forms of energy is essential. This will provide sufficient time for entrepreneurs and public officials to increase investment in innovative technology and in new transport infrastructure. It will also allow time for the cultural changes that will be required to convince the general public to use and value renewable, non-polluting forms of energy even if it costs more than fossil fuel.

Since Northern countries are the main culprits in polluting the atmosphere they must give a lead in transforming the energy base of modern society. Furthermore, because the energy habits of Northerners have a global impact and will cause massive suffering in many Southern countries, a percentage of green taxes collected in the North should be made available to help clean energy and energy efficiency in the South. The South should also be compensated for the fact that, because they are not highly industrialised, they produce a very small percentage of the total global greenhouse gas emissions. One could argue the case that the North should compensate the South for not producing CO_2.

If the South follows the industrialising pattern of the North global warming problems will escalate dramatically. The thought of a thousand million Chinese driving around in cars in two or three decades does not bear entertaining. Yet they have the same rights as First World people to enjoy prosperity and affluence. In other words, global warming raises serious questions about whether the present development model is just or sustainable. If the worst effects of global warming are to be avoided, we must cut down the use of fossil fuel by sixty per cent.

Is effective political action on the horizon?

I began this chapter by pointing out that the issue of global warming is not high on the daily agenda of the average person, despite the fact that it is probably the most serious global environmental problem. Governments are beginning to take the first tentative steps towards tackling this difficult issue. Climate change figured prominently on the agenda of the United Nations Conference on Environment and Development, popularly known as the Earth Summit, that took place in Rio de Janeiro in June 1992. After eighteen months of negotiations, 154 countries signed the Framework Convention on Climate Change. The purpose of the Convention was to reduce eighteen greenhouse gas concentrations in the atmosphere to a level that would prevent dangerous anthropogenic interference with the climate system. The effectiveness of the Convention was undermined when the US administration pandered to their powerful fossil fuel lobby and refused to set specific targets for reducing carbon dioxide emissions.

A slight change in the US approach to global warming took place with the election of President Clinton. By 1996 the Clinton Administration began to talk about taking global warming more seriously. As a result, the parties to the UN Convention on Climate Change, which met in Geneva in July 1996, produced a strong statement committing industrialised countries to negotiate a legally binding international protocol to reduce their greenhouse gas emissions. The targets set in the Declaration of Geneva were modest, but they represented a step in the right direction.

Much of the debate and political manoeuvring around global warming came to head during the UN Conference on Climate Change in Kyoto, Japan in December 1997. While the scientists who are members of the Intergovernmental Panel on Climate Change insist that a 60 per cent cut in greenhouse gases is needed to stabilise the climate, all that the participants at the Kyoto meeting could agree to was to reduce carbon dioxide emissions by 5.2 per cent by the year 2010. The European Union was willing to be more co-operative but the U.S. set its face against any comprehensive or radical response.

Opposition to taking action on global warming

Since global warming has the potential to cause massive pain to human beings and destruction to the earth, every individual and institution should do what they can to halt it. Unfortunately, many transnational corporations (TNCs), especially those involved in the energy sector, instead of tackling global warming, have lobbied hard to prevent any effective treaty limiting greenhouse gas emissions. They are afraid of losing hefty profits if there is a drop in the use of fossil fuel. Some of these companies have questioned the scientific consensus on the greenhouse effect. They have promoted the work of people like the Australian scientist, Patrick Michaels who has poured cold water on greenhouse predictions. They quote his work and urge caution, demanding that no action should be taken that might have an adverse impact on business, until further research has confirmed that global warming is a fact. In the meantime they advocate a business-as-usual approach. They fail to point out that Micahels's research has, in part, been funded by the Cyprus Mineral Company, Edision Electric Institute and the German Coal Mining Association (*The Guardian*, 29 October 1997).

Governments, under pressure from industry, have also adopted this sceptical, wait-and-see approach. US Vice-President Albert Gore, in his book, *The Earth in Balance*, recalls that in the run-up to the Earth Day celebrations in 1990, the Bush Administration advised its spokespersons not to deny that global warming might be a problem. Instead they were to focus on the many uncertainties in global warming research in an effort to forestall a groundswell of opinion which might insist on effective controls for fossil fuels and CO_2 emissions.

Energy-intensive industries are particularly opposed to the introduction of a carbon tax. The Dutch government's proposal to introduce an energy tax in 1992 drew the wrath of many transnational companies based in Holland. Energy-intensive companies like the petrochemical giant Shell, the steel company Hoogovens, the KNP paper mill and chemical producers like Akzo, DSM and Dow, attacked the proposal vehemently as undermining their international competitiveness. Furthermore, they threatened to close their plants and move investment out of Holland to countries like Kazakhastan if the government proceeded with its plan. In the face of such blatant blackmail it is difficult for individual governments to introduce a carbon tax unless other industrialised countries like Japan and the US also adopt such measures. Securing such a consensus is not easy. In March 1992 the then EC environment commissioner, Carlo Ripa de Meana, failed to persuade the EC Environment ministers to introduce a carbon tax to stabilise CO_2 emissions at 1990 levels before the Earth Summit at Rio (*The Guardian*, 20 March 1992, p. 31).

It is worth mentioning that the insurance industry has begun to challenge the foot-dragging and stonewalling approach of the fossil fuel industry. Insurers like Lloyds of London and Re of Munich have linked events like Hurricane Andrew, which hit Florida in 1992, with global warming. In recent years they have paid out huge amounts in compensation for weather-related disasters. In 1992 alone insurers paid out $23 billion for storm and weather damage and the costs are rising every year.

Kyoto 1997

In the run-up to the Kyoto Conference on global warming in December 1997, a group of industries known as the Carbon Club ran an advertisement campaign in the United States to forestall any major cuts in greenhouse gas emissions. The campaign was extremely effective and put huge pressures on the US delegation at Kyoto not to concede too much. The dominant group in the Carbon Club was the Global Climate Coalition. This was very much a Who's Who of U.S. business and industry. It included such names as Esso, Shell, Ford, General Motors and the leading coal, steel, aluminium and energy corporations of the US. They ran a $10 million campaign of TV ads 'designed to scupper the climate treaty with dire warnings that jobs would be lost and taxes would rise if a meaningful treaty went ahead'.

Paul Brown, writing in *The Guardian* (29 October 1997), pointed out that the aim of the PR exercise was 'to sow enough doubts that the politicians would not feel they needed to act. Using corporate PR, psychology, mass media manipulation techniques and political muscle to get to the politicians and opinion formers they set up a series of front groups, funded "independent scientists", nurtured politically conservative and far-right think-tanks, and sought to discredit individuals and, especially, environmental groups at every turn. With money no object they could run rings around their opponents'. These tactics proved successful. The Byrd-Hagel resolution passed earlier in 1997 urged the US Senate not to ratify any treaty that might damage the US economy. The resolution was passed in the US Senate by a majority of 95 to 0.

True to its free-market ideology, the US administration was more interested in including mechanisms for 'emissions-trading' rather than reducing its greenhouse gas emissions. This idea would enable countries like the US with large greenhouse gas output to buy 'credits' from poor countries in Africa, for example, that have lower emissions. Many old power plants in the Eastern Europe or Russia are very inefficient. The 'emission-trading' concept would allow a US company to invest in improving the efficiency of these dirty plants rather than spending

the money fixing up a plant back home. This market mechanism, designed to buy one's way out of greenhouse gas difficulties, did not meet with a favourable response from either Third
World countries or the environmental organisations (*The Guardian*, 11 December 1997, p. 17). Third World countries would like
to see a large-scale transfer of clean-energy technology from the
North to the South to help alleviate global warming.

At Kyoto the US also indicated that it would not agree on
limiting greenhouse gases unless developing countries also
begin to cut their greenhouse emissions. The double digit
growth rates in the Chinese economy during the past decade
and a half have meant that China's carbon dioxide emissions
have risen steeply (*The Guardian*, 10 December 1997, p. 4). In
reality, of course, the impact of the US energy policy far out-
weighs that of poor countries. Each individual in the US uses 5.4
tonnes of carbon dioxide each year. The comparable figure for
India is 0.3 tonnes per head (Paul, Brown, *The Guardian*, 4
November 1998, p. 4.)

Ireland

During the Kyoto meeting the media focused on those countries that were most strongly opposed to reducing emissions,
namely the US, Australia and oil-producing countries of the
Middle East, such as Saudi Arabia and Kuwait. Ireland, as a
small and until recently a predominantly agricultural and rural
society, was not one of the major producers of greenhouse
gases. For that reason, in a burden-sharing package, the European Union, in the run-up to the Kyoto meeting, agreed that the
cap on Ireland's greenhouse gas emissions would be 15 per cent
above the 1990 levels.

With the growth of the Celtic Tiger economy in the 1990s all
of this has changed. One would have thought that, given the
prominence of global warming at the Earth Summit in 1992,
Ireland might have made strenuous efforts to curb CO_2 emis-

sions. In fact, CO_2 output increased by 10 per cent between 1990 and 1997.[9]

A study by the Economic and Social Research Institute (ESRI) in 1997 predicted that unless present energy policies change dramatically Ireland's greenhouse gas emissions will rise 28 per cent above 1990 figures by the year 2010. This judgement is based on the fact that Ireland's GDP will grow by an average of 5 per cent for the next decade and a half.

Environmental groups like EarthWatch and VOICE (Voice of Irish Concern for the Environment) have been very critical of the Irish Government's energy policy. Sadhbh O'Neill of EarthWatch has been particularly critical of the government. In an article in *EarthWatch* (Autumn/Winter) 1998 she lists fourteen different areas where present government policies have contributed to increasing greenhouse gas emissions. Top of the list is the fact that the present government has authorised the building of a peat-fired power plant in Edenderry in the midlands instead of investing money in wave or wind energy. The 120 megawat peat-fired plant will emit 634,000 tonnes of carbon dioxide into the atmosphere each year, increasing our contribution to global warming. It seems that the Bord Pleanála decision to allow the generating station did not have to consider the environmental impact of the operation. This comes under the remit of Environmental Protection Agency, according to Frank McDonald in *The Irish Times* (26 December 1998, p. 11).

Putting huge investment into fossil fuel energy sources while neglecting renewable energy sources is very short sighted. It is generally recognised that Ireland has enormous potential for developing both wind and wave energy, but initiatives in these areas have been curtailed because of lack of capital investment. The Irish Wind Energy Association has estimated that 10 per cent of Irish energy needs could be supplied by wind energy by the year 2010 if a suitable policies were pursued by vigorously by the government. Sadhbh O'Neill has proposed that the government should set a target of 20 per cent of renewable energy by 2010. She argues that such a target should be imposed on all those energy suppliers who plan to enter the deregulated electricity market. Unless such targets are set, suppliers will not invest in alternative energy technology.

O'Neill also claims that the Environmental Protection Agency (EPA) is not promoting alternative energy initiatives. The EPA granted an integrated pollution control (IPC) licence to Aughnish Alumina in the Shannon estuary to continue burning fossil fuel with high sulphur dioxide emission. The IPC licence only required Aughnish to investigate rather than implement cleaner, more efficient power-generating methods such as incorporating combined heat and power technology (CPH).

Regarding transport, the government has delayed the light rail system for Dublin known as LUAS. O'Neill points out that Dublin's public transport is ranked among the most underfunded in Europe. In the late 1990s the frequency, reliability and comfort of the public transport system was way below par; and, therefore, it did not appeal to many commuters who still preferred to use their cars. Countrywide, very few resources have been spent to improve public transport (rail and bus). Little work has been done to provide safe bicycle lanes, segregated from other traffic and facilities to park bicycles securely in urban areas. Every town in the country should be made bicycle-friendly.

The Irish government has been slow to encourage, through tax incentives or grants, energy conservation in homes and other buildings.

What should the Church do?
What role, if any, have the Churches to play in responding to the reality of global warming? Given the seriousness of the issue

and the potential for disaster for the poor of the world, it must be addressed with urgency and long-term commitment. Despite the fact that it is seldom mentioned by religious leaders it is obvious that the Churches have an important role to play in forming peoples' consciences and putting pressure on industrial and political leaders. Global warming is, in the language of Vatican II, a 'sign of the times'. The Council was convinced that the Church must interpret these phenomena or events in 'the light of the Gospel, if it is to carry out its task' (*Gaudium et Spes*, n. 4).

Thus, the Churches, in their determination to witness to the truth, must take a prophetic stance for justice and the integrity of God's creation. There are two elements to this prophetic stance. The first is to assess and evaluate thoroughly the scientific evidence for global warming and the impact it is likely to have on people, especially the poor, future generations and on the planet itself.

If the Church community is convinced that global warming is taking place then, in the light of the Gospel of Jesus, it must challenge the people and institutions who are primarily responsible for global warming, to change their affluent lifestyle and their wasteful use of energy. This aspect of prophecy is in continuity with the prophets of the Hebrew Scriptures. Amos, for example, thundered against the lifestyle of the women of Samaria whose extravagant demands 'oppressed the needy and crushed the poor' (Amos 4:1).

The second aspect of prophecy moves beyond critiquing and condemning unjust social, economic and political structures. It attempts to liberate the imagination of individuals and Christian communities and empower them to seek new ways of living that will be just, non-polluting and sustainable. If Christians simplify their energy demands and support renewable energy initiatives they will be following the injunction of Yahweh in the book of Micah 'to act justly, to love tenderly and to walk humbly with your God' (Mic 6:8).

Pope John Paul II on global warming

How effectively have the Churches carried out their prophetic mission? Ecological issues did not figure prominently in Catholic social teaching until the publication of the encyclical *Sollicitudo Rei Socialis* in 1988. It took another two years before the issue of global warming was dealt with. Pope John Paul II in his January 1, 1990 message, *Peace with God the Creator, Peace with All Creation*, wrote:

> The gradual depletion of the ozone layer and the related 'greenhouse effect' has now reached crisis proportions as a consequence of industrial growth, massive urban concentrations and vastly increased energy needs. Industrial waste, the burning of fossil fuels, unrestricted deforestation, the use of certain types of herbicides, coolants and propellants: all of these are known to harm the atmosphere and environment. The resulting meteorological and atmospheric changes range from damage to health to the possible future submersion of low-lying lands. While in some cases the damage already done may well be irreversible, in many other cases it can still be halted. It is necessary, however, that the entire human community of individuals, states and international bodies take seriously the responsibility that is theirs. (n. 6).

In the latter part of the document, the Pope shows a keen understanding of the fact that reducing energy use will demand drastic and even painful economic and political changes. He writes: 'simplicity, moderation and discipline, as well as a spirit of sacrifice, must become part of everyday life, lest all suffer the negative consequence of the careless habits of a few' (n. 13).

While *Peace with God the Creator; Peace with All Creation* shows an accurate understanding of the reality of global warming and its likely impact on people, the Pope's analysis is not very detailed and there is little enough guidance as to what individuals or communities might do. It is also true to say that this document or the wider ecological challenges are not very prominent in the contemporary teaching or witness of the Catholic Church at either a global or local level. Everyone knows the Catholic Church's stand on a range of sexual matters. Few people, even Catholics are aware that the papal magisterium has addressed the religious and ethical dimension of environmental degradation.

The work of the World Council of Churches

A much more detailed examination of global warming has taken place within the World Council of Churches (WCC) culminating in the publication, in May 1994 of the document mentioned above Accelerated Climate Change: Sign of Peril. Test of Faith.[10] The WCC has been concerned about environmental issues since the Nairobi Assembly in 1975. In 1988 it sponsored a consultation on global warming attended by Church members, environmental groups, scientists and politicians. During the following years the WCC continued to share with its member Churches the significance of global warming both as a threat to the well-being of God's creation and as a justice issue involving North/South relations. WCC observers took part in the meetings that led to the adoption of the UN treaty on climate change at Earth Summit in Rio de Janeiro in 1992.

In the wake of the Rio meeting the WCC observers presented an assessment of the treaty and made a number of recommendations. Firstly, they felt that it was important to deepen theological and ethical reflections on climate change. Secondly, they saw the importance of letting people know that responding to climate change would involve profound changes in all spheres of life. Thirdly, the ecological, economic and political aspect of climate change ought to be assessed from a justice perspective, especially in the light of the growing gap between the North and the South. And, finally, they understood it was crucial to provide the Churches with a resource base on these reflections to assist them in their work of education and advocacy.

Sign of Peril, Test of Faith addresses this agenda. Chapter 1 evaluates the scientific evidence for global warming and attempts to predict the consequences. It accepts that, while there are some uncertainties in the scientific data, it would be irresponsible in the light of the 'probable serious consequences for humans and life in general' to delay a response. The document supports the adoption of the 'precautionary principle' contained in the Framework Convention on Climate Change (Art. 3.3). This requires political authorities to support strict environmental measures to avoid potentially damaging consequences even in the absence of totally conclusive scientific evidence linking greenhouse gas emissions with global warming.

Chapter 2 develops a theological and ethical framework for interpreting global warming by Christians. These reflections flow from basic tenets of the Christian faith – God's love and concern for creation and the poor of the world; the propensity of humans to disobey God's will and inflict pain on people and creation; and awareness that God's grace can move people to repentance. Faced with the problems of global warming, repentance ought to involve a willingness to opt for a new way of life based on simplicity and sufficiency rather than endless, greed-driven accumulation of material possessions.

Reflection on God's care for and sovereignty over creation reminds Christians that our ethical behaviour is not confined to action that affects other human beings, but that a violation of creation is also a sin. Then there is the justice dimension of the way people in different parts of the world have used fossil fuel. One fifth of the world's population have an insatiable appetite for fossil fuel and are responsible for 85% of greenhouse gas emissions. On the other hand the poorest 20 per cent of the world's population need to increase their use of energy to enjoy the basic necessities of life. Aside from the inequities involved in the distribution of global energy resources, the present consumption level of non-renewable sources of energy deprives future generations of their fair share of the earth's resources. In summary, the theological and ethical reflections affirm that God loves the whole universe and calls on human beings who are presently oppressing other human beings to abandon the arrogance and greed that endangers creation's future.

Chapter 3 looks at what a positive response to global warming might mean for the various sectors of society. It attempts to spell out what might be involved for industry, especially TNCs trading in goods and services. There is a short reflection on the implications of a clean energy policy for military establishments around the world. If Kuwait was only renowned for growing carrots and had no oil reserves it is doubtful that Northern military led by the US and Britain would have mobilised to liberate it from Iraqi invasion in the early 1990s. The document also looks at how issues like deforestation and population growth might be addressed. The document is adamant that any comprehensive response to global warming will involve profound changes at social, political and economic levels in every part of the world.

Chapter 4 discusses how countries might schedule a realistic timetable in order to reduce their production of greenhouse gases. This chapter and the following one recognise that the response from the affluent North and the impoverished South will obviously need to be very different. People have a right to adequate food and the basic necessities of life, but they do not have a right to waste energy or abuse the earth. Governments and industry must pursue policies that promote energy efficiency and accelerate the shift from fossil-fuel to energy derived from a combination of sources – wind, solar, micro-hydro, tidal.

Chapter 6 raises the crucial question: Can the targets for emissions be met within the present global socio-political system where economic growth is extolled as the panacea for all problems, especially overcoming poverty in the Third World and unemployment in the First World? The document questions the growth strategy and reminds readers that unlimited economic growth in a world of finite resources is manifestly impossible. On the larger planetary scale, coping with global warming requires that the rich must live more simply so that the poor may simply live. The drafters of the document are not naive. They realise that the changes they are calling for will not happen without major changes in global priorities. They also recognise that governments are primarily responsive to the rich and powerful elements of society, whose interests are tied to the present growth-oriented system.

Chapter 7 argues that reducing the threat of global warming will require a new vision of what constitutes the good life. Such a vision will seek to transform our relationships with other human beings and motivate us to live in harmony with the rest of creation.

Chapters 8 and 9 examine the potential role of the Churches in addressing the crisis of accelerated climate change. They sketch the contours of an appropriate global justice, peace and integrity of creation spirituality. In line with the Churches' prophetic vocation to denounce evil and empower Christians to seek the path of reconciliation and harmony, the report argues that the Churches must actively campaign on the global warming issue in co-operation with independent environmental organisations.

The crucial question of Northern lifestyles is also addressed: Are not the comforts that many people consider essential today a careless exploitation of nature and unsustainable in the long-term? The authors remind Christians of old ways of living in Christian history characterised by simplicity, discipleship, and worship and adoration of the Creator of all life.

I have dwelt at length on the document, *Signs of Peril, Test of Faith*, because I believe that the methodology used and the message it proposes are as relevant to the Catholic Church as they are to member Churches of the WCC. Its analysis of global warming is competent, both from a scientific and a theological perspective, and its recommendations are appropriate and well thought-out. It suggests a viable programme for action as a way of responding to one of the most important contemporary ethical question.

It is significant that in March 1996 the President of the Pontifical Council for Justice and Peace, Cardinal Roger Etche-garay, writing to the Presidents of the Episcopal Conferences of industrialised countries, acknowledged that the World Council of Churches has 'taken a leading role in drawing the attention of its member Churches to the relationship between climate change and human activity'. He encouraged local Catholic Churches to examine ways in which they could co-operate with any WCC-inspired initiative in their country.

Personally I would like to see the document disseminated widely in the Catholic Church so that, at global and local level, the Catholic community might assume its God-given responsibility to witness to the life-giving, good news of Jesus in our time.

CHAPTER FOUR

God called the waters 'seas' and saw that it was good

Why worry about the oceans that are so vast and therefore seem impossible to harm? The answer is very simple. Without the oceans our planet would be as barren and inhospitable as Mars. There would be no meadows, no forests, no birds, animals or people. Life on earth began in the oceans over three thousand million years ago and was nurtured there for over one thousand million years before it began to colonize the land. When life did come ashore it brought the oceans with it. Water makes up approximately 70 per cent of any living being, including human beings. At this point in history the waters of the earth are under threat from human activity.

UNESCO proclaimed 1998 as the International Year of the Ocean. The purpose of the Year was to 'obtain commitments from governments to take action, provide adequate resources and give priority to the oceans and coastal areas which they deserve ... ' One might have expected stories, comment and analysis about the threats facing the oceans from a combination of reckless exploitation and human indifference. Right up to the end of 1998 there was little substantial coverage of the problems facing the oceans that surround this island or sustain life globally apart from a few reports in *The Irish Times* during the OSPAR convention on marine pollution which took place in Portugal in mid-July.

Our 'water' planet

We call our planet earth because our culture views the planet from a land-based perspective. If an astronaut had been asked to name the planet he/she would probably have called it water. It is abundantly clear from space that 70 per cent of the planet's surface is covered by water. Most of this water is found in the oceans.

We know more about the surface of the Moon and Mars than we do about what happens at the deepest parts of the oceans. Researchers have studied less than 10 per cent of the ocean because of the difficulty of penetrating its deepest recesses. In 1996 there were only 20 robots or submersibles capable of transporting people beyond even half the ocean's deepest regions which in a number of places on the planet reaches 11 kilometres.

The ocean contains not only most of the planet's water but also a very diverse range of living organisms. About 300,000 marine species have been identified, but it is commonly held by marine scientists that there is at least double that amount of species. Some scientists believe that the ocean floor alone may contain up to 10 million species.

Destructive pressures

It is tragic to think that much of this marine life may be destroyed long before it is ever identified by humans. The pressure on the oceans comes from industrial pollution, mounting population pressures along coastal zones, and fishing methods which are akin to strip mining. There are about thirty-five major seas in the world: some are coastal, and some are enclosed by land. Seven of these seas – the Baltic, Mediterranean, Black, Caspian, Bering, Yellow, and South China Seas – have been seriously damaged in recent decades. In a single year the Yellow River can dump 751 tons of cadmium, mercury, lead, zinc, arsenic and chromium into the South China Sea along with 21,000 tons of oil. The pulp and paper mills of Sweden and Finland which now supply 10 per cent of the world market, also deliver 400,000 tons of chloride compounds into the Baltic Sea each year.

The inland seas fare much worse. The water of the Black Sea, once a flourishing eco-system, is now 90 per cent dead. Each year the Danube dumps an estimated 60,000 tons of phosphorus and 340,000 tons of inorganic nitrogen into its waters. It has little chance of being flushed clean since it takes 167 years for the water from the Danube delta to reach the Mediterranean, and much longer to reach the Atlantic.

One symptom of the damage done to the Caspian Sea, by the Volga's highly contaminated water (and over-fishing), is the almost total collapse of sturgeon fishing (the source of caviar) along the southern Iranian shore. It has fallen from 6,700 tons in 1960 to half a ton in some recent years.

Because the bulk of marine life everywhere is found close to the coast, even localized pollution can cause enormous damage. Two marine eco-systems are particularly vital for a vibrant and healthy marine environment. These are the coral reefs and mangrove forests. Both eco-systems have been under attack for decades and now are in a precarious state globally. The 600,000 square miles of coral reefs in the planet's tropical and subtropical seas are the marine equivalent of the rain forests. They are home to one million species of fish, crabs, fish, eels, molluscs, worms, sponges, grasses and algae.[1]

The toll on coral reefs and mangrove forests

A study coordinated by the University of Hong Kong in 1997 found that coral reefs around the world are in a lamentable state. The results of the research makes very depressing reading. Researchers checked 300 reefs in 30 countries and found that a mere 32 per cent of the reefs had living coral cover. That meant that 69 per cent were barren or seriously degraded. The Caribbean had the lowest rate of living coral at 22 per cent. South East Asia was just a little better with 30 per cent living cover. During my twenty years in the Philippines in the 1970s and 1980s I came to love the magic of coral reefs with their richness of life and striking pastel colours. At the same time I was saddened to witness the widespread destruction of coral reefs through siltation from deforestation and monocrop agriculture, and through destructive fishing methods which included the use of cyanide and dynamite. The developing tourist trade is also having a negative impact on the health of the corals.

Even in Australia the Great Barrier Reef which runs for 1,284 miles along the east coast is under threat because of rising ocean temperatures caused by global warming and because of pollution. The fact that coral are dying in such numbers ought to act as a wakeup call to humans to recognize that the oceans are sick. If no remedial action is taken in the near future, dying and polluted oceans could have dire, irreversible consequences for the future of the planet.

Mangroves, found in the same areas as corals, are the breeding and nursery ground for vast numbers of fish. They are one of the most productive life systems on earth. Yet here again it is a story of massive destruction. Over the past century 25 million hectares of mangrove forests have been destroyed. Thailand has lost 27 per cent of its mangroves, Malaysia 20 per cent, the Philippines 45 per cent and Indonesia 40 per cent. The expansion of commercial fish farming in these countries in the 1980s contributed considerably to the destruction of the mangroves. UNESCO experts believe that Indonesia's recent decision to make a further 840,000 hectares available for such business will have a disastrous impact on fishing in the area. My experience in the Philippines was that these fish farms were a disaster for the poor. Generally they produced shrimp and expensive fish for export. In doing so they destroyed the mangroves and depleted the natural fish stocks for poor fishermen.

Stripping the oceans bare

Over-fishing is depleting the oceans and leaving them barren. Many people felt that the oceans were so vast and the variety and supply of fish so abundant that there would always be vast quantities of fish in the sea. We are now learning how false those assumptions were. According to a report by the UN Food and Agriculture Organization (FA0) in 1995 over 70 per cent of the world's marine fish stocks were either 'fully-to-heavily exploited, over-exploited, depleted, or slowly recovering'.[2] The depletion is most notable in many of the world's most productive fishing grounds. These include the Grand Bank of Canada and New England. Cod fishing has collapsed in the North Sea.

Most of the damage to the oceans has been done in this century. Fish catches have increased by a staggering twenty-fold, from three metric tons at the beginning of the century to almost 90 million in 1989. Most of the increase happened after World War II when sonar and radar tracking technologies that had been developed for military purposes, were now used to locate and catch fish. Furthermore, super-trawlers the size of a football field were built to accommodate nets thousands of feet long. In a single netting these boats can take up to 400 tons. The modern trawler can remain at sea for months at a time and is equipped to freeze and process the catch. Their fishing methods are so indiscriminate and destructive that a huge percentage of the catch, deemed unsuitable for commercial purposes, is simply dumped back into the oceans. Worldwide, it is estimated that 27 million tons or more than 25 per cent of the total annual catch are thrown away, because they are the wrong size, sex or species. These throwaways (known as bycatch) are a main cause of the disastrous drop in the North Sea herring population.

The fact that a sizable portion of the annual catch consists of immature fish means that the breeding stock is being decimated. This will inevitably mean smaller catches in the future. It is now clear that since World War II what can only be described as a war on the fish species of the world has been pursued relentlessly.

The net result is that global fish catches peaked in 1989. They have been falling ever since. In 1998 they were down over 30 per cent despite improved gear, tracking and snaring technology and the fact that more species at different depths in the ocean are being targeted. Given present trends it is inevitable that there will be further decline if not an outright collapse of fishing worldwide. Daniel Pauly the author of a new study on global fishing trends predicts that 'if things go unchecked, we might end up with a marine junkyard dominated by plankton'.3 To date, policy makers and fishing fleet owners have ignored the numerous stock assessments carried out either at a national or international level. Dishonesty and corruption are rife. Between 1986 and 1992 more than six times the quota for cod, flounder and redfish were taken from the Grand Bank off the Canada coast. When Spanish ships were boarded by Canadian police in 1995, the Canadians found two sets of books on board. One recorded the true tonnage of the catch for the owners. The other books – with false, reduced figures – were meant for the authorities when the ships were challenged.

It is essential that human beings begin to recognize that the destruction of the oceans impoverishes the planet for all future generations. The main losers in the human community are 200 million small scale fishermen in Third World countries and fishermen in coastal regions in First World countries. These have lived for generations off the catches they have made around their native shores. Fish has also helped to feed these communities and has often provided the main source of food, especially, protein.

Giant trawlers plunder the seas

At present many of the huge trawlers, responsible for the slaughter of creatures of the oceans, are heavily subsidized by governments. The subsidies take different forms – from providing fuel tax exemptions to low interest loans or outright grants for boat building and equipment. For example, in recent years Don Tyson, the Arkansas chicken magnate, received $65 million in low interest loans from the US Federal Government to build ten super-trawlers.

It is these kind of subsidies that have skewed the economics of global fishing to a remarkable degree. At present it costs approximately $124 billion annually to catch $70 billion worth of fish. The huge short-fall is bridged by governments. It is because of these subsidies that fishing can be a lucrative business for the large-scale operator.

On the other hand the present policies are driving the small scale operators out of business. Once the coastal waters are fished bare small scale fishermen are forced out of business. Unlike the wealthy owners of multi-national fishing fleets they cannot operate far from shore and, furthermore, they do not have the money to invest in some other profitable business once fish stocks collapse. If the livelihood of small fishermen, who provide much more employment than the large-scale competitors, is to be protected it is essential that the subsidies to factory fish operators, which are destructive both socially and ecologically, be discontinued. This will not be easy to achieve. It will take a lot of courageous political action at local, national and the international level.

Problems from industrial and agricultural waste

As if all this were not enough humans are also polluting the oceans with industrial waste that includes heavy metals, organochlorines (such as DDT and PCBs) nuclear waste and agricultural effluent. Thirty to fifty million metric tons of untreated or partially treated sewage are released into the Mediterranean each year. In the Third World it is much worse. In Nigeria, over 60 million litres of raw sewage flows into lagoon in which Lagos is situated. In the Indian sub-continent the cities of Calcutta and Bombay between them dump 765 million metric tons of sewage and waste into the oceans each year while Karachi pollutes the Arabian Sea with 175 million tons of sewage and industrial waste.

The destruction wrought by industrial, chemical and radioactive pollution is not confined to the coastal areas in which it is dumped. It can be carried around the world by ocean currents. DDT and PCBs, for example, have turned up in the fatty tissue of seals in the Arctic and penguins in the Antarctic. In the past fifty years or so over 70,000 chemical compounds, pesticides, cleaning agents, dioxins and pharmaceuticals have entered the global environment. Radioactive technetium 99 which is discharged from the Sellafield nuclear plant in Cumbria, has been found in increasing concentrations along the Norwegian coast.

There is increasing evidence that chemical pollution poses a very serious threat to the survival of Cretaceous like whales and dolphins. Even low-level contamination can increase their susceptibility to disease and decrease their level of infertility. In the longer term this could lead to disaster. Ms Sian Pullen, head of the marine unit of the World Wide Fund For Nature (WWF), in the run up to the OSPAR conference stated that 'some of the most exotic sea creatures around Irish and British coasts, and some hundreds of species in total, are threatened by large-scale dumping of industrial chemicals, heavy metals and oil pollution'.[4]

The ubiquitous plastic bag also causes damage and great suffering to marine life. To a turtle, a plastic bag bobbing up in the ocean looks like a jellyfish. Once consumed the plastic blocks the turtle's intestine and causes a slow, painful death.

Agricultural effluent is also a problem. Run-off of nitrogen and phosphorous has led to an increase in nutrients in rivers, lakes and seas and a subsequent explosion of phytoplankton. This in turn depletes oxygen in the waters and causes eutrophication. The North Sea, the Baltic Sea, the Black Sea and the Gulf of Mexico have been particularly affected. It has led to die-back in sea-grass meadows, an increase in algal blooms and a consequent decline in fisheries. Scott W. Nixon writing in *Scientific America* (Fall 1998, p. 51) assert that 'oxygen depletion cuts a lethal swath through some 18,000 square kilometres [7,000 square miles] of the deep waters of the Gulf of Mexico every summer, creating a barren region called the "dead zone".' Enriching nutrients may also cause toxic varieties of phytoplankton to bloom. These in turn contaminate the shelf fish that feed on them.

We need to care for the oceans

For ages, the sea has taken care of human beings. We now know that we are intimately connected with the oceans. If the oceans become toxic our food and our bodies will also become toxic. The time has come for humans to start taking care of the sea. We need to move quickly and comprehensively. Only 20 of the 177 countries that have coastlines have implemented effective coastal management plans. To combat over fishing there is a need to limit the kind of technology that is allowed in fishing and to create protected areas where fishing is simply not allowed.

To stop marine pollution will mean rigorously enforcing the Oslo Convention on dumping waste and toxic substances at sea which was ratified as far back as 1972. This was followed two years later by the Paris Convention on dumping from land sources. This includes radioactive waste. Both these conventions were merged to form OSPAR in 1992. The OSPAR Convention requires the contracting parties to take all possible steps to prevent and eliminate pollution.

The OSPAR ministerial statement that emanated from the

Sintra Conference in Portugal in July 1998 adopted strong measures to protect the marine environment. It included a commitment to reduce radioactive waste to as close to zero as is technically feasible by the year 2020. The environmental organization Greenpeace saw this as the death knell for the nuclear reprocessing plant at Sellafield in Cumbria. Other commentators, like the Irish Labour Party spokesman, Emmet Stagg, were not so sure. He felt that the clause 'as is technically feasible' is a classic let-off strategy for British Nuclear Fuels Ltd (BNFL).[5]

The Sintra Convention also prohibits the dumping of oil rigs at sea unless it can be proven that this will not cause environmental problems. This is also a significant ruling in the light of the controversy which surrounded the decision by Shell Oil to dump the oil rig the *Brent Spar* at sea a few years ago.

There needs to be more political pressure to persuade companies to abandon the production of polluting chemicals and move instead towards clean production techniques which would end the dumping of toxic substances into the ocean. But as Bruce McKay, a researcher for Sea Web, writes: 'change will not come easily. Much of humanity has developed a profound dependency on nitrogen-based fertilizers, fossil fuels pesticides, and a host of other environmentally damaging goods and services'.[6]

On a global level the provisions of the Convention on the Law of the Sea, that was negotiated in the early 1980s and came into force in 1994, need to be enforced more rigorously. The enabling bodies, like the Tribunal for the Law of the Sea, require adequate funding and competent staffing. Given the pressure on the oceans globally – from fishing, from oil and gas exploration and from dumping – the traditional notion of 'freedom of the sea' will have to be abandoned. There is a pressing need for more appropriate management policies for the high seas.

The ocean in the Bible

Because the Israelites were not seafaring people like the Phoenicians or the Vikings the oceans get very little mention in the Bible. This is in stark contrast to the wealth of material on land. Normal Habel in *The Land is Mine* argues that there are at least six biblical perspectives on land.[7] Animals, both domestic and wild, and birds also figure prominently in the Scriptures.[8]

The oceans, on the other hand, seem to be on the periphery of Israelite cultural and religious consciousness. Pious Jews would automatically expect to experience Yahweh's power on land, whether in the desert, the mountain, the vineyard, the farm, the city or especially the Temple. In Psalm 107 the author argues that this power is also encountered in unexpected places, namely the oceans. 'Others, taking ship and going to sea, were plying their business across the ocean; they too saw what Yahweh could do, what marvels on the sea' (Ps 107:23-24)

In this Psalm and in Genesis 7:11f; 9:11.15 the ocean is not seen as a benign, human-friendly place. Rather the fearsome nature of the ocean and the fragility of the seafarers riding in small fragile boats is emphasised, 'He spoke and raised a gale, lashing up towering waves. Flung to the sky, then plunged to the depths, they lost their nerve in the ordeal, staggering and reeling like drunkards with all their seamanship adrift' (Ps 107:25-27). Jonah's trip from Joppa to Tarshish, the lone sea journey of the Old Testament, reinforces this negative image of the sea as a dangerous place, possibly not far from the gates of the underworld (Jon 2:7). In Job the sea also symbolizes evil because it is seen as the home of the sea monster (Job 7:12).

Even in the New Testament the sea is presented as a dangerous and even demoniac place. The demons that terrorised the Gerasene demoniac beseeched Jesus to allow them to enter the swine who then 'charge over the cliff into the lake, and there they were drowned' (Mk 5:13). Mark portrays Jesus as having power over the sea. At the height of the storm his 'Quiet now! Be calm' caused the wind to stop and quietness to reign (Mk 4:39).

The sea as a dangerous and threatening place can function as a metaphor for any kind of personal danger. In Psalm 69 the Psalmist, recognizing he is in difficulty and facing grave danger, feels that 'I have stepped into deep water and the waves are washing over me' (Ps 69:2b).

In the Hebrew Scriptures there appeared to be a pervasive fear that the waters might invade the land (Prov 8:29). In response to this, Yahweh was seen to display both his power over all the elements, even rebellious ones like the oceans, and his concern for the people – imposing limits to the seas at the dawn of creation (Gen 1:9f). Even Psalm 104, which is one of the most insightful and observant pieces of natural history writing in the Bible still shares the ambivalent attitude towards the oceans. Only Yahweh's word can keep the waters in check: 'You imposed limits they must never cross again or they would once more flood the land' (Ps 104:9; Job 38:8-11).

The underlying fear evoked by the ocean is even present at the end of the New Testament in the vision of the future portrayed in the Book of Revelation: 'Then I saw a new heaven and a new earth, the first heaven and the first earth had disappeared now, and there was no longer any sea' (Rev 21:1). As we saw earlier, we now know that an earth without the sea would be cold, barren, miserable and, most of all, lifeless.

There is, of course, a more positive approach to the oceans in the Bible. The oceans are created by God (Gen 1: 9-10). Because they are God's creature the Psalmist invites the 'oceans and all that move in them' to praise God (Ps 69:34). We find the same theme in the Song of the Three Young Men: 'Seas and Rivers! bless the Lord' (Dan 3:78).

As Christians, living in a world where the oceans are under

threat from human activity, we need to develop this positive strand in the biblical teaching in order to shape a positive theology of the oceans. Such a theology will help give us energy and support us in our efforts to protect the seas in today's world.

Because the biblical view of the oceans is both scant and ambivalent we will need to augment this with the positive understanding of the place of the oceans in our world which has become available to us through the research of modern sciences. This story of the earth or more correctly, story of the waters of the planet ought to become the basis for this new understanding and regard for the oceans. The stories and myths of various maritime peoples, like the following Eskimo song which expresses their delight and love for the oceans, can be woven into the new caring attitude towards the oceans.

> The Great sea has set me in motion,
> Set me adrift,
> And I move as a weed in the river.
> The arch of the sky
> and the mightiness of storms
> Encompasses me,
> And I am left
> Trembling with joy.

CHAPTER FIVE

We All Live Downwind from Hiroshima and Chernobyl

On August 6, 1945 at 8.15 a.m. when bombardier Tom Ferebee released the trigger on the gun-sights of *Enola Gay* as it flew over Hiroshima he ushered in a new era in human and planetary history. Forty-three seconds later a thunderous fireball exploded, torched the city and spawned a lethal mushroom cloud. The scale of human slaughter was unprecedented and horrendous. More than 70,000 children, women and men died instantly. A further 50,000 died excruciatingly painful deaths within the next few weeks and months as a result of radiation poisoning.

Five days later another atom bomb exploded high above the Catholic Cathedral of Nagasaki adding a further 70,000 victims to the carnage that marked the birth of the atomic age.

This 'butchery of untold magnitude' (Pope Paul VI, 1976) continues to mar and haunt the lives of the *hibakusha* (survivors). Many suffer from cancer, especially leukemia. A survivor from a rural village in Nagasaki bewailed the particular plight of young women. 'Nobody's going to marry those Nagasaki girls. Ever since the bomb fell, everybody's calling them "the never-stop people". And the thing that never stops is the bleeding. Those people are outcasts – damned, untouchable. Nobody is going to marry one of them ever again'.

In a very real way we are all *hibakusha*. We live today in a world downwind from Hiroshima, Nagasaki and Chernoybl where the air, water and soils have been contaminated. The atmospheric nuclear tests conducted by the US, the Soviet Union, Britain, France and China between 1945 and 1980 have contaminated the air and the upper atmosphere. The groundwater and aquifers of the Great Basin of the US contain radioactive nuclides from underground nuclear testing at the Nevada test site. Many rivers and even the oceans are awash with nuclear waste. Lakes near Hanford in Washington State and Ghelyabinsk in the former USSR are so polluted that Geiger counters spin off the scale. The earth itself is scarred with both strip and open-pit uranium mines. More recently, areas in a number of countries have been designated 'national sacrifice zones' because the contamination is expected to last for tens of thousands of years.

The most frightening scenario for a nuclear disaster at the moment is in Russia. This country which is collapsing economically and socially has a stockpile of over 1,500 tons of nuclear fuel. Unfortunately, there are not sufficient resources to guard the nuclear material. Many people fear that, unless this material is safely disposed of, the Russian nuclear powder keg could explode with devastating consequences for all life on earth. Given the poverty of so many professional people in Russia there is real danger that they might sell off radioactive material like plutonium to the highest bidder. In 1993 the going rate for plutonium was $800,000 a kilogramme. According to Frank Barnaby, a British nuclear physicist and former director of the Stockholm Peace Institute, this would be enough material for a group of skilled technicians to make a crude nuclear device. Even if the resulting explosion was only equivalent to a few tonnes of TNT it could 'completely destroy the centre of a large city'.[1]

The nuclear weapons programme distorted the economies of the US and of Russia and even the global economy. In the end, it bankrupted the USSR and led to the present collapse. It is estimated that the US spent over $31 billion on nuclear weapons each year during the 1980s and early 1990s. This amount of money would clean up fifteen of the worst national hazardous waste dumps, send 263,000 children to the Head Start programme for one year, fund completely the vaccine research for AIDS for one year and hire an extra 42,000 police.[2] The clean-up cost for US nuclear weapons facilities is expected to top $200 billion and will take thirty years to complete. Far from guaranteeing global security, the nuclear strategy threatens to undermine and destroy it.

The nuclear burden falls heavily on the poor

While everyone in the world and the earth itself have paid a terrible price for nuclear weapons production, it is ironic that the people who have paid the highest price are often tribal peoples whose cultures have promoted harmony between human beings and the rest of creation. Although only about two-thirds of US uranium deposits lie within reservation boundaries, as much as 90 per cent of the country's mining and milling operations have taken place in or close to Indian lands since the early 1950s.

In July 1979 the largest radioactive spill in US history took place at the United Nuclear mill at Church Rock, New Mexico. 100 million gallons contaminated the drinking water for over 1,700 Navajo people and their livestock. In the aftermath of the accident the company refused to supply emergency food and water. Rather than attempting to minimize the damage, the corporation stonewalled for nearly five years before agreeing to pay a paltry $525,000 out of court settlement to its victims.[3]

Between 1952 and 1958, nuclear bomb tests were conducted by the British Government at Emu fields and Maralinga in Northern Australia, contaminating large areas of Aboriginal sacred lands and causing radiation sickness in Aboriginal families. The sufferings of the Aboriginal people went largely unnoticed. It was only in the 1980s when British and Australian ex-servicemen who were present at the tests began to die from cancer that the British government agreed to an inquiry. In a landmark decision Britain agreed to pay Australia $30 million to clean up the Maralinga site though this is less than half of the true cost as estimated by the Australia government.

Between 1966 and 1992 France carried out forty-four atmospheric tests and more than 100 underground blasts at the Moruroa and Fangataufa atolls in Te Ao Maohi (Tahiti). The French government claims that these tests have not harmed the environment have been contradicted by numerous scientists. The American scientist Norm Buske, using data from Jacques Cousteau's brief 1987 survey of Moruroa, found an abundance of caesium 134 (a radioactive isotope produced only by nuclear reactions) in the Mururoa lagoon. This suggests that nuclear underground tests leak radioactivity into the marine environment within one-and-a-half to five years.

Political and religious leaders in Oceania and the Pacific reacted with outrage to President Jacques Chirac's decision, on June 13, to resume underground testing at the Moruroa atoll in September 1995. Cardinal Pio Taofinu'u in a pastoral letter to Samoan Catholics called the planned tests 'a sin against the people of the Pacific'. He charged that France would 'rape with nuclear explosiveness the people, lands and seas of the South Pacific'. In solidarity with the peoples of the Pacific, the cardinal encouraged individuals and governments around the world to bring maximum pressure to bear on the French government to abandon their path of nuclear madness.

In recent years numerous political and religious leaders – including former President Mary Robinson and Pope John Paul II – as they stood at the cenotaph in Hiroshima and contemplated the horrors of August 6, 1945, have appealed to humanity to abandon nuclear weapons before it is too late. Unfortunately, in 1998 the testing of nuclear weapons by India and Pakistan enlarged the nuclear club for the first time since 1964. The street carnival atmosphere and jubilation that greeted the

tests among some sections of the Indian and Pakistani population were thoroughly depressing. Newspapers in both countries carried photos of demonstrators with placards welcoming
nuclear tests. Politicians exploited the nuclear test to gain
instant popular support. They spoke about the events in terms
of vindicating national pride. There was very few reflections on
the horrendous dangers posed by the dawn of the nuclear age
on the Indian subcontinent. India and Pakistan have fought
three wars since independence from Britain in 1947. There are
still areas of potential conflict especially around the disputed
territory of Jammu and Kashmir. The fact that both countries
now have nuclear weapons in their arsenals adds to the possibility of a nuclear conflict in South Asia.

The nuclear tests by India and Pakistan were condemned by
the other nuclear powers, especially the US, Britain and France.
But the nuclear tests in South Asia underscores the hypocrisy of
these nations. For decades these countries have paid lip-service
to the Nuclear Non-Proliferation Treaty. Article VI committed
the parties to undertake nuclear disarmament, end the nuclear
arms race, and conclude a treaty on disarmament. This applied
to all the states that possessed nuclear arms at the time – China,
France, Russia, the United Kingdom and the United States of
America. Non-nuclear arms countries that signed the treaty
committed themselves to renouncing the right to manufacture
or acquire nuclear arms. The countries that possessed nuclear
weapons were never really committed to the disarmament
dimension of the treaty. What they really want was to ensure
that nuclear weapons do not fall into the hands of other nations,
especially those in Asia or the Middle East.

Ireland played a prominent role in proposing and framing
the Nuclear Non-Proliferation Treaty (NPT). Many were disap-
pointed that the Irish voice on nuclear disarmament was not as
clear and univocal when the Treaty can up for re-negotiation in

1995. France held the presidency of the European Union at the time. Ireland supported the French position on the Treaty despite the lamentable record of France on nuclear testing.

The fact that Ireland sponsored a motion on nuclear disarmament on December 4 1998 may indicate that the Irish government has returned to its robust anti-nuclear stance. This is one area where our commitment to our partners in the European Union, especially the nuclear-armed states Britain and France, must not be allowed to dilute our resolute anti-nuclear stance. The motion was adopted overwhelmingly by the General Assembly of the United Nations: 144 countries voted in favour of the motion, 18 against and there were 38 abstentions. Implementing this motion ought to be a top priority for people everywhere and, especially, Christians, as we move into the next millennium. There must be no mistake about it. The presence of nuclear weapons anywhere on the globe is a threat to life on earth. Unless humans defuse this arsenal there is every possibility that nuclear weapons will destroy humanity.

Problems with nuclear power generation

The dangers of nuclear power are not confined to nuclear weapons. On 26 April 1986 the worst human-created nuclear and ecological disaster took place at a nuclear power station in Chernobyl. The explosion hurled 190 tons of uranium and graphite into the atmosphere. This radioactive material was carried by the wind all over Europe. The most immediate effect was to bring ruin, devastation and desolation to the lives of millions of people, especially those living in Belarus, Western Russia and the Ukraine.

Initially, the Soviet authorities tried to cover up the incident. There is nothing unusual in that ploy. Governments worldwide have consistently misled the public about the nature and dangers of nuclear power. The British took over thirty years to tell the full truth about the 1957 accident at Windscale, while for thirty-seven years the US Government covered up the release of radioactive iodine at the Hanford Nuclear Reservation. The Soviet authorities waited nineteen days before issuing a statement on Chernobyl. The statement seriously minimized the long-term impact of the explosion by claiming that only thirty-one people had lost their lives in the tragedy. In recent years, however, the real levels of human suffering and death caused by Chernobyl are beginning to emerge. It is a picture of gross deception, incompetence and exploitation that has resulted in horrendous suffering for millions of people. And, unfortunately, the worst may be yet to come.

The first people to suffer from Chernobyl were a group of men called the 'liquidators'. Initially robots were used to remove radioactive graphite from the damaged reactor's core. When the robots failed, 600,000 men were conscripted to clean up the mess. Were it not for 'liquidators' like Lt Col Shuklin, the helicopter pilot who flew above Chernobyl directing those who poured cement on the stricken reactor, the fire would have spread to the other reactors, causing far worse damage locally and globally. These men were not properly briefed on the dangers of nuclear radiation; and, as a result, many wore minimal protective clothing and were therefore exposed to massive doses of radiation. Col Shuklin is now suffering from radiation sickness. Ms Adi Roche in her book, *Children of Chernobyl*, estimates that 13,000 'liquidators' have already died and a further 70,000 are permanently disabled. In 1986 these men were hailed as national heroes. Today those who remain alive are suffering from crippling radiation diseases and, by and large, have been forgotten by the state.

The 'liquidators' were not the only victims of Chernobyl. Hundreds of thousands of people were forced to leave their towns and villages within a thirty-mile radius of Chernobyl.

This was not a temporary exile. These people are permanently excluded from the homeland where their ancestors have lived for hundreds of years. Tens of thousands of people, especially children, have developed a variety of cancers, notably of the thyroid gland. Radiation has also weakened their immune systems. As a result a growing percentage of all children living in the area have developed liver, kidney and stomach diseases.

The deadly blight of Chernobyl also fell on the land in the surrounding countries. An area equivalent in size to England and Wales, from what was once known as the bread basket of the Soviet Union, is so contaminated that food cannot be grown there until the end of the next century. It is not as if the land has been torched or degraded in a way that is clear for everyone to see. The awful reality is that the land looks lush and fertile, but it bears within itself a cocktail of invisible and deadly radio-active elements. Ten years after the accident the average life-span for Belarussians had fallen by four years and there was a significant rise in incidences of lung and stomach cancer. Diseases of the immune system have also rise sharply in number.

Lakes and rivers in the area are contaminated. Radiation has already reached the Black Sea. Fish have been caught with 400 times the concentration of caesium-200 found in similar fish elsewhere. Vegetation and livestock have also been affected.

The poisonous cloud of Chernobyl spread further afield. Thousands of miles from the Ukraine, on the island of Benbecula in the Outer Hebrides radioactive fallout from Chernobyl has been blamed for a dramatic rise in the number of cancers. Widespread radioactive contamination was detected around Ireland in the days following the explosion at Chernobyl. This contamination, mainly iodine-131, caesium-134 and caesium-137, resulted from persistently heavy rain that washed the radio-active material out of the atmosphere into the soil. The most affected areas were the mid-lands, the border area and

Ulster. Dublin recorded a 30 per cent increase in radioactivity. Experts disagreed on the health impact of the contamination. Professor Ian McAulay, associate professor of physics at Trinity College, stated 'that there was no detectable radiation effect on health'. Dr Mary Dunphy of the Irish Medical Campaign for the Prevention of Nuclear War disputed this. According to her no base-line data such as a register of miscarriages existed before 1986. She advised young people and pregnant mothers against drinking fresh, possibly, contaminated milk.[4]

Ten years after Chernobyl the affects of the disaster were mainly felt in the sheep sector. In Derry and Antrim 15,000 sheep on 57 farms must still be tested for radiation before being sold. The figure in Wales is much higher, running at 220,000 sheep and in Scotland the figure is 76,000.

The spectre of another disaster is ever-present at Chernobyl and at numerous nuclear plants in central and eastern Europe. The sarcophagus that was built to entomb reactor 4 at Chernobyl is disintegrating at an alarming rate. Kathy Sheridan writing in *The Irish Times* (13 April 1996) reports that it now has holes big enough to drive a car through. Scientists now admit that many of the fifty-eight nuclear power stations operating in the former Warsaw bloc countries have serious flaws in the design and construction process. As in the case of Chernobyl, safety features are often disregarded and monitoring procedures are inadequate. The former Swedish Prime Minister, Carl Bildt, has called for the closure of forty of these plants. However, owing to the strength of both the local and global nuclear and industrial lobby, the plants are still in operation despite the dangers.

The accident at Chernobyl was the result of faulty technology and human error. The potential for human error is a crucial factor in the whole nuclear debate. The nuclear industry is very aware of this and knows that public support for nuclear power has dropped dramatically since Chernobyl. Very few nuclear power plants have been built in Europe or the US since Chernobyl. Instead of critically analysing whether nuclear power is an appropriate form of energy for our world, the nuclear industry has mounted a massive public relations campaign, often at taxpayers' expense, to woo people back to support nuclear power.

The aim of the exercise is to convince a sceptical public that nuclear power is safe and that Western nuclear technology can clean up and make safe the nuclear dinosaurs that dot the landscape of the former Warsaw bloc countries. This PR spin overlooks the fact that a near catastrophic accident took place at Three Mile Island in Pennsylvania in 1979. It also conveniently forgets that in 1983 an official of the International Atomic Energy Agency (IAEA, which operates as a pro-nuclear lobby), assessed the Chernobyl-type reactor and judged that 'a serious accident with a loss of cooling is practically impossible'. IAEA's record after the explosion was also very poor. They sponsored a study into the health impact of Chernobyl entitled 'The International Chernoybl Project'. But, as Kathy Sheridan reports in *The Irish Times*, while the study found there was plenty of ill-health it claimed that none of it 'could be traced to Chernobyl's door'.[5] The article goes on to quote a British scientist and a World Health Organisation study that indicate that one in every four of young children who live in the most contaminated area can be expected to develop thyroid cancer. To put it in context, the usual expected number is one in a million.

Given the history of nuclear power and the dangers associated with it, which are graphically revealed by Chernobyl, the crucial question that should to be addressed is whether the human community ought to commit itself irrevocably to a technology with such far-reaching and irreversible consequences. The more nuclear technology proliferates, the greater the possibility that a Chernobyl accident will happen else-

where, especially when nuclear technology is exported to countries where there is insufficient scientific and technological
knowledge and training to handle it responsibly. Neither can
one overlook the possibility that, given the widespread unrest
in the modern world, terrorist groups may target nuclear installations or attempt to obtain plutonium in order to create their
own crude weapons. Significant amounts of plutonium, suitable for making nuclear weapons, have been smuggled out of
the former Soviet Union in recent years. As Scott Sullivan of
Time Magazine put it: 'Ever since the end of the cold war and the
collapse of the Soviet Union, scientists have warned that the
vast quantities of radioactive material stored in Russia and
other former Soviet republics were loosely accounted and
badly accounted for'.[6]

It is ironic that in recent years nuclear power has been
presented as 'Green' energy, and therefore, the perfect solution
to the greenhouse problem. In August 1994 Nuclear Electric
took out a full page advertisement in the *Sunday Times* proclaiming: 'We don't contribute to global warming. We don't
contribute to ozone depletion. And we don't cause acid rain.
Are we friends of the earth?'

This is the latest phase of a multi-million-pound PR campaign to promote nuclear power. In the early years of the
industry, in the 1950s, the pro-nuclear lobby argued that it was
safe, cheap and reliable. All these claims have been proved to be
false.

Nuclear power is expensive
It is now agreed that nuclear power is more costly than power
generated from conventional methods – oil or coal – and is
much less versatile. In an article in *The Ecologist* Jim Jeffrey
disputed the claims by the Central Electricity Generating Board
(CEGB) in Britain that nuclear energy is cheaper than energy

from fossil fuels. Jeffrey maintains that electricity produced in coal-oil burning stations is significantly cheaper. For many years in Britain the CEGB used misleading accounting methods to maintain that nuclear-generated electricity was cheaper than that generated from coal. Finally, in 1987, the Chairman of the CEGB admitted that nuclear power had not been cheaper after all. When the price of decommissioning nuclear plants is factored in the costs rise astronomically. Most revealing of all, in July 1993, Sir John Bourn, head of the National Audit Office in Britain, warned Members of Parliament that the total cost of decommissioning and reprocessing was 'a financial time bomb'. He estimated that the total cost could be as high as £40 billion.[7]

The expansion of nuclear power will create environmental, health, economic and security risks. Nuclear power is dangerous at every stage of the industry's operation, from the mining and milling of uranium to the disposal of nuclear waste. Unfortunately, the volume of these poisonous wastes is increasing every year, For example, by 1986 the eleven uranium mills in the United States alone had accumulated 191 million tonnes of tailings on the ground. There is a growing fear that radioactive and chemical poison from this material will seep into the ground-water and permanently contaminate it. At the Hanford installation 422,000 gallons of radioactive liquid waste leaked out of the storage tanks. Tritium has been detected in ground-water, strontium-90 has been found in the Columbia river and plutonium in the nearby soil.

People working in nuclear power stations also face many health hazards. A report released in Bonn in 1987 by a committee composed of workers, trade union representatives and the proprietors of the nuclear industry recommended that certain types of cancers should be recognized as occupational diseases for workers in nuclear plants.

The nuclear burden will continue to haunt humanity and the

earth community for centuries as some of the elements are lethal for up to 250,000 years. Many people feel that it is a crime against future generations to develop nuclear power extensively and encourage its proliferation when no safe way has yet been found to store and dispose of nuclear waste. E.F. Schumacher, author of *Small Is Beautiful*, insisted that 'no place on earth can be shown to be safe for the disposing of nuclear waste'.

Sellafield and Thorp

The main nuclear dangers to Ireland are posed by the nuclear power station at Sellafield in Cumbria and the building of the £2.85 billion Thermal/Oxide Reprocessing Plant (Thorp) in the early 1990s. During the past 45 years there has been over 700 accidents and incidents at Sellafield. The accidents range from a serious fire to minor problems. The worst incident took place in 1957. A fire broke out at one of Sellafield's two reactors. The fire was brought under control within twenty-four hours but a radio-active material did escape. In 1983 radio-active waste was accidentally released into the Irish Sea. The British Department of the Environment warned the public not to use nearby beaches for six months. In September 1992 thirty litres of plutonium leaked from an evaporator causing the reprocessing plant to be shut down. Initially, the company said the closure would be for only a few days. In fact that plant remained close for two months. In April 1997 British Nuclear Fuels was fined the maximum £20,000 at Whitehaven Magistrates Court under the Radioactive Substance Act. The fine was levied because a bridge carrying nuclear waste pipelines over a railway line in Cumbria was in such poor repair that it could have collapsed on the passenger train.[8]

THORP increases the level of danger to Ireland dramatically. The idea of recovering spent fuel was conceived in the aftermath of the oil crisis in 1973. It was assumed that there would be a dire shortage of oil, coal and gas. However, THORP would enable Britain to meet its energy needs from recycled uranium and plutonium. The military would also benefit. Some of the seven tonnes of plutonium that would be recovered each year could subsequently be used for making nuclear weapons. Though THORP has not operated at full capacity it has the potential over its life-time to produce 59 tonnes of plutonium which is enough to make 6,800 bombs. Paul Leventhal of the Nuclear Control Institute in Washington wonders who will 'guarantee the safety, security and peaceful use of this extraordinary material during its shelf-life of hundreds of thousands of years'.[9]

Given the potential for destruction, especially, for Ireland, a country that has forsaken the development of nuclear power, building and operating the plant seems grossly immoral. The Radiological Protection Institute of Ireland has estimated that THORP will increase the radiation doses to the most exposed members of the Irish people by 20 per cent. The Institute points out that this will still only amount to 0.2 per cent of a person's total annual radiation from all sources.[10]

While the plutonium will be around for hundreds of thousands of years much of the logic for building the plant has, in fact, crumbled in less than two decades. Uranium today is as cheap as it was in 1973. New gas and oil fields have come on stream since 1973 that are expected to last for four or five decades. The economics of recycling nuclear material have also collapsed as many countries feel that it is cheaper to store spent nuclear fuel than to have it recycled. Finally, in the post- Cold War era even the military find it hard to justify building more nuclear weapons.

Because THORP poses such a danger to people living on the east coast of Ireland the High Court gave permission to a group of residents in Dundalk to bring a case against British Nuclear

Fuels Limited, the company that operates both Sellafield and THORP. The plaintiffs claim that 'they are being subjected to hazardous emissions of noxious and poisonous materials emanating from BNFL's nuclear plant'.[11]

Problems with storing nuclear waste in Eastern Europe and the former Soviet Union

The storage of nuclear waste is causing alarm in eastern and central Europe. There are six reactors at Kozloduy in northwest Bulgaria, close to the Danube. Inspectors from the International Atomic Energy Agency (IAEA) in Vienna found that the pools in which the radioactive spent fuel rods were being cooled were in a deplorable state. Before the collapse of the Soviet Union, spent fuel was shipped there for reprocessing and storage. Installations in Russia will now accept spent fuel only if the service is pre-paid in US dollars. Local currencies are not acceptable. As a result dangerous a stockpile is building up, housed in totally inadequate facilities. Ivan Uzunov, a physicist and adviser to the Bulgarian Parliament's Environmental Committee, reported: 'we now have 700 tons of spent fuel elements resting in swimming pools ... If these ponds are breached because of an earthquake or some other accident, the spent fuel could melt down.' Uzunov continued: 'It would cost us $1 billion to have the spent fuel reprocessed or stored in France, but we cannot afford it, we simply can't spare the foreign exchange'.[12]

Limited energy resources raise serious questions about whether our present industrial society is sustainable in the long-term. Fossil fuels are limited in quantity, but so is uranium. Only by opting for fast-breeder reactors can uranium resources be stretched to meet even a percentage of the future projected needs of a continually expanding industrial society. However, choosing the stop-gap method of nuclear power means meeting our present energy needs in a way that puts at risk every succeeding generation of living organisms on planet earth.

The Catholic Church and civilian nuclear power

Given the havoc that nuclear power has wrecked on the lives of peoples and on the fertility of land in the vicinity of Chernobyl it is difficult to understand the position which the Holy See has taken on nuclear power in recent decades. In an address to the International Atomic Energy Agency (IAEA) in Vienna on September 12, 1982, the Vatican representative, Mgr Peressin stated that:

> The peaceful uses of nuclear energy has both advantages and disadvantages. The advantages of the very application of nuclear energy, whether in agriculture, food preservation, medicine or hydrology were widely recognized. The most important sector, however, was that of energy production for industrial and domestic use at a time when energy sources were becoming increasingly rare and energy production costs were rising. Nuclear power could contribute to the economic development of Third World countries and could help prevent the dangerous phenomena of deforestation and desertification due to excessively intensive exploitation of non-renewable energy sources. The benefits of peaceful uses of nuclear energy should thus be extended to all countries, in particular to developing countries....
>
> The use of nuclear power did, however, involve risks, associated either with accidents that might arise at nuclear power stations or with the storage of radioactive waste. Certain groups of naive idealists and even certain personalities from the scientific, political, cultural or religious worlds condemn the use of nuclear power simply for that reason. It seems more realistic not to overlook any efforts to guarantee the safe operation of power stations and the safe disposal of

wastes and to minimize thereby the risks incurred on the understanding that, as with any human enterprise, it was impossible to eliminate them totally. This delegation there-fore welcomes the expansion of the Agency's nuclear safety programme; thanks to the efforts which has been made in that regard no fatal radiation accident had occurred at any nuclear facility operated for non-military purposes. These efforts should be pursued, especially, as far as the long-term storage of radioactive waste was concerned, and informa-tion for the public should be more extensive and more complete with a view to preventing the creation of an atmos-phere of fear and distrust.[13]

Apart from it being insulting to anti-nuclear campaigners, the most charitable comment on this statement, especially in the light of Chernobyl, is that it is remarkably naive. Almost every claim in the statement is open to serious question. As we have seen, nuclear power is very expensive, especially when one includes decommissioning costs.

Unfortunately, eleven years after that statement the Holy See was still promoting what is called peaceful use of nuclear power. In an address to the General Conference of the Interna-tional Atomic Energy Agency on September 26th, 1993, the Vatican representative Archbishop Donato Squiccianrini chose to ignore the appalling nuclear disaster that had taken place at Chernobyl and continued to promote nuclear power. He stated:

The Holy See believes that all possible efforts should be made to extend to all countries, especially to developing ones, the benefits contained in the peaceful use of nuclear energy.[14]

It is ironic that the Holy See which is constantly promoting pro-life values should so easily be co-opted by the nuclear lobby to promote a form of energy which has created a hell on earth for the people of Chernobyl and, to a lesser extent, on a global level. Nuclear power is not the solution for the energy needs of

Third World countries. When the Bataan nuclear plant was being built in the Philippines a group of concerned Filipino scientists wrote to the then President, Mr Marcos, asking him to abandon the project.

> We believe in the intellectual endowments of our Filipino scientists and engineers. Given the opportunity for research and funds to conduct studies in nuclear physics, we know that they will be more than capable. But such research, funds and training are not available in the country today. In the case of any accident, we feel that we will not yet be in a position to cope with the situation. Nuclear technology is not our field. We hope it never will be.

Despite the pro-nuclear rhetoric that has obviously been accepted by the Vatican, nuclear power will not be a financial Godsend for Third World countries. In fact the main beneficiaries are First World corporations who sell their nuclear technology to Third World countries. In the Philippines, for example, the initial estimate for the cost of the Bataan nuclear plant put the figure at $600 million. As a result of the Chernobyl disaster construction at the Bataan nuclear plant was suspended in April 1986. At that point the cost had already reached £2.2 billion – a fourfold increase.

Thankfully, not everyone in the Vatican has been seduced by the promoters of nuclear power. Cardinal Arinze, of the Pontifical Council for Inter-religious Dialogue, in his message to the worldwide Muslim community on the global ecological crisis at the end of Ramadan in 1995 mentions the 'dangers caused by industrial and nuclear waste should also be mentioned'.

Choose conservation and renewable energy
Chernobyl was a massive blow to the pro-nuclear power lobby. It slowed down dramatically the construction of nuclear power

stations around the world. Its impact was probably most widely felt in the United States. No commercial nuclear reactor has been built in the United States for almost twenty years. There has also been a significant slowdown in building nuclear reactors in Europe. Many governments, including Spain, Switzerland, Finland and Sweden, have effectively placed a moratorium on the construction of new reactors. Even in France, where, for decades, nuclear power was energetically promoted by the government, nuclear power is on the wane. This will most probably accelerate since Green Party members opposed to nuclear power joined both the French and German governments in the late 1990s.

Asia is the only continent where nuclear power is still being vigorously promoted, but even there the signs are that confidence is beginning to erode, both because of technical difficulties and the cost base. In December 1995 when sodium coolant leaked from the Fast Breeder Reactor in Monju in Japan the nuclear industry attempted to cover up the full extent of the damage. This, and other incidents, has led to an erosion of public confidence in the industry.

Chernobyl marked a defining moment for civilian nuclear power. In the year of the accident, 1986, there were 430 commercial nuclear power stations operating around the world and another thirty were under construction. Since then, numbers have been falling with eighty reactors being permanently shut down. At that time nuclear power accounted for only 17 per cent of global electricity out-put. Present indications are that this figure will fall further in the next few years. Still, the pro-nuclear lobby argues that since fossil fuels are limited, the world will need nuclear power to supply energy in the post-fossil fuel era. This argument fails to acknowledge that uranium is also limited. Only by opting for fast-breeder reactors can the uranium resources be stretched to meet even a percentage of the future projected needs of a continually expanding industrial global society. While accepting the need for a comprehensive and effective energy policy it would be insane to meet our present energy needs in a way that puts at risk every succeeding generation of living organisms on planet earth.

The present and future scarcity of energy should spur humans to do two things. Firstly, to look at ways of conserving energy in all that we do today. Secondly, to develop alternative means of producing energy from non-polluting sources – the sun, the wind, biomass and water. For example, research into photovoltaic cells is proceeding rapidly. There is a need for more resources to be made available to research and promote these non-pollutant forms of energy. The World Bank Report of 1992 put the present dilemma in focus. It noted that only 6 per cent of public research funds was used for research into renewable sources of energy while 60 per cent was devoted to research into nuclear power. The reason, of course, is that the nuclear power industry wields enormous political power and it can easily access public finances.

Even in 1999 the industry wants the West to invest $580 million dollars in building two nuclear stations in the Ukraine. The argument is that this will allow the remaining reactors at Chernobyl to be shut down. The real reason according to Paul Brown is that building nuclear power plants in Eastern Europe will bail out 'companies in the West's ailing nuclear industry'.[15] If the project goes ahead it will be ironic that the huge subsidy to the nuclear industry will come from European taxpayers' pockets, most of whom are opposed to the nuclear industry. Hopefully, opposition from citizens and environmental groups will scuttle this profligate waste of money. The common good of human beings and the planet demand that such wasteful ventures be stopped and the money be used for alternative sources of energy.

In the wake of the accidents at Chernobyl, Three Mile Island and Sellafield and the continuing problem of dealing with nuclear weapons and waste, people are rightly fearful of nuclear power. These fears are real and one would like to see that the authorities in the Catholic Church took them seriously.

I find it very difficult to understand how Christians who believe that the earth was created by God and is sustained by God can support a form of energy that will remain lethal for tens of thousands of years. The Bible and Christian tradition affirm the goodness of creation and challenge human beings to be good stewards of creation. Because nuclear energy creates radioactive waste, for which there is no safe means of disposal, wise stewardship must surely preclude this option for Christians. Furthermore, it is irresponsible to create and operate a technology that has the potential for accidents like Chernobyl.

I would argue that those who believe in preserving the integrity of God's creation must join together to change direction before it is too late. To stop the fire at Chernobyl in 1986, Reactor 4 was enclosed in concrete. For the American journalist Don Hinrichsen this concrete 'sarcophagus' is a fitting symbol to the nuclear energy venture, in its civilian and military phase, that is now, hopefully, dying.

CHAPTER SIX

Ethics and Genetic Engineering

Unease among environmental organisations and the general public about the safety of genetically engineered foods surfaced in Ireland in 1997. In response the Minister for the Environment, Mr Noel Dempsey, T.D., promised in January 1998 that his department would shortly publish a consultation paper on genetic engineering. The document entitled, *Genetically Modified Organisms and the Environment*, finally appeared in August 1998. It purported to be an objective, evenhanded document, explaining what genetic engineering is and outlining the national and European Union regulations governing the release of genetically engineered organisms or the sale of genetically engineered food. However, as many in the non-government organisations (NGO) community feared when the 'consultation' process was announced, the document was heavily weighted in favour of the industry's point of view.

From the very first page the use of the term 'traditional' and 'modern' biotechnology gave the impression that there is an inevitable evolution and continuity between traditional breeding practices that were restrained by species boundaries and the radical techniques involved in recombitant DNA technologies. Those who opposes the deliberate release of genetically engineered organisms at this time dispute this claim. That should have been acknowledged in an unbiased report.

Furthermore, the critics of genetic engineering are calling for a genuine public debate about all aspects of this new, extraordinarily powerful technology before the public are swamped by food products containing transgenetic plants or animals. Those opposed to the present commercially driven pressures to get genetically engineered products to the market want to scrutinize the technology thoroughly. This is quite understandable since the technology has the power to reshape the world of nature and human nature itself in a most radical way. Governments ought to facilitate such a scrutiny; they are elected to protect the common good.

The Consultation Paper was not the kind of root-and-branch assessment one might expect given what is at stake. It is little more than a revision, updating and reworking of regulatory guidelines, many of which are totally inadequate. The paper naively asserts that biotechnology has the potential to 'support economic growth and employment creation' without analysing who will benefit most and lose most if the technology assumes the dominance which the biotech industry is seeking. I will argue that the main beneficiaries will be a handful of giant agribusiness and biotech companies who in the process will secure a monopoly over many of the staple crops of the world.

Such concentration of economic power in the hand of the few for something as important as our food raises serious questions about equity and sustainability. It certainly will not benefit the vast majority of humankind living in the Third World or even small and medium size farmers in the First World. The document does not mention the fact that in 1997 the Mississippi Seed Arbitration Council ruled that Monsanto's genetically engineered RoundUp Ready cotton failed to perform as advised and as a result recommended that the farmers receive $2 million compensation for their losses.[1]

The fears and anxieties which have arisen as a result of the biotechnology revolution were accurately captured in a joint statement by Minister Dempsey and his colleague, Joe Walsh, the Minister for Agriculture, both of the Fianna Fáil party, while in opposition on 26 April 1997. They argued that 'it is premature to release genetically modified organisms into the environment or to market food which contain any genetically modified ingredient ... ' The reason for such a stand was very simple:

'Fianna Fail will not support what amounts to the largest nutritional experiment in human history with the consumer as guinea pig'.

Though not explicitly stated, this is fundamentally an ethical argument. It is significant that the word 'ethical' only appears twice in the seventy-six-page Consultation document on pages 7 and 47. In neither case was there any effort to develop an ethical framework or enunciate principles that might be helpful in assessing this powerfully intrusive technology from an ethical perspective. Such an oversight, in a country where over 90 per cent of the people subscribe to the Christian tradition with its strong ethical core, is difficult to explain. This chapter will attempt to address some of the ethical issues involved in genetic engineering.

Widening the framework for ethics

To develop an appropriate ethical framework for this new and powerful technology which can literally transform not just human life but life itself, will demand a major shift away from the almost exclusively human or homocentric focus which has been so pervasive in the Western ethics and wider cultural traditions for almost two thousand years.

Aristotle, whose impact on Western thought is enormous, held that since 'nature makes nothing without some end in view, nothing to no purpose, it must be that nature has made (animals and plants) for the sake of man'.[2] This idea that animals and plants are created for humankind – either by God or the processes of nature – has dominated western attitudes to animals, plants and the rest of creation for many centuries.

From this viewpoint, since animals and plants exist for human beings, our behaviour towards them is not governed by moral considerations. It is only in the past decade that the cruelty involved in factory farming or blood sports has been discussed from an ethical perspective. Even then the proscription on cruelty towards animals arises, not so much from inherent rights that animals might have, but from the understanding that any form of cruelty is unbecoming and, therefore, unethical for rational beings.

Certain elements within the Judeo-Christian tradition have strongly reinforced the Aristotelian legacy. This is particularly the case when one considers the traditional interpretation given to Genesis 1: 26-28. 'Increase and multiply and dominate the earth'. The text is often interpreted, mistakenly according to contemporary Scripture scholars, as giving humans a licence to dominate the earth and do whatever they wish with animals and plants.

The historian, Keith Thomas, points out that at the beginning of the sixteenth century, just as modern science was finding its feet, neither Western literature nor the theological tradition ascribed any intrinsic meaning to the natural world or accorded it any rights apart from its role in serving humankind.[3] From the theological perspective it was argued that humans had intrinsic value because they were made in the 'image and likeness of God' (Gen 1:26). Their role was to be 'masters of the fish of the sea, the birds of heaven and all living animals on the earth' (Gen 1:28). No other creature bore this *imago Dei* stamp. Animals and plants were viewed as lacking rational faculties, self-consciousness and often even sentience and hence as having no intrinsic worth in themselves. They only had instrumental value: their role was to serve the needs of humankind for the necessities of life and they could also be used for entertainment.

It is true that within the Judeo-Christian tradition there is a strand that sees humans as stewards of creation (Gen 2:15). Unfortunately, as Clive Ponting points out in his *Green History of the World*, 'although the idea that humans have a responsibility to preserve the natural world of which they are merely guardians can be traced through a succession of thinkers it has remained a minority traditions'.[4] Unfortunately, St Francis's kinship with brother Sun, Sister Moon and all creation was very much a minority position. His fraternal attitude did not inform the Western approach to nature. In fact it did not even survive in any effective way within the congregation which he founded.

The gulf between humans and the rest of creation was widened further by the insights of many of the people who have shaped our modern scientific, economic and social world. In this very formative period in human-earth relations when the foundations of the modern scientific and industrial society was being shaped in the works of people like Francis Bacon (1561-1626), René Descartes (1596-1650) and Isaac Newton (1642-1727) all rights were ascribed to humans. In the words of Descartes the goal of human knowledge and technology was so that humans might become 'the masters and possessors of nature'.[5] Furthermore, philosophers like Thomas Hobbes, John Locke and Jeremy Bentham dismissed the medieval view of the cosmos as organic and substituted instead a mechanistic view of nature and its law. For these men the best way to understand the cosmos was to see it as a giant clock. Newton believed that the laws of motion, which he discovered, proved that the same 'universal laws that governed the smallest portable watch also governed the movements of the earth, the sun and the planets'.[6]

For Descartes animals were *res extensa*, little more than mechanised entities without any interior quality or soul. Only *res cogitans* or humans, as conscious beings, were endowed with souls and therefore could be considered to have moral value. Because animals had no such intrinsic value they could be treated in any way that might serve human ends, no matter how cruel and degrading that treatment might be. Moreover, these men of the Enlightenment viewed science, and its handmaiden technology, as tools designed to give humans the power to dominate and manipulate the earth in whatever way they saw fit in order to promote human well-being and betterment.

Genetic engineering fits comfortably into this mechanistic world-view. Scientists, working in genetics and biotechnology discovered the insights and technology which people like Francis Bacon dreamed about in his book, *New Atlantis* (1627) published after he died. This new technology gives humans the capability to manipulate the building blocks of life in order to reshape the natural world in a most extraordinary way. Most of the questions surrounding genetic engineering deal with whether it will be damaging to human health or the environment. In general the wider ethical questions are often simply ignored.

A hierarchy of moral questions
The fundamental question is whether genetic engineering respects the intrinsic rights of other creatures. Having explored that question one might then move on to some of the other ethical questions associated with the technology. Are the risks to the environment and human health from genetic engineering serious enough to warrant a moratorium on deliberate release of genetically modified organisms at this time? Within the context of the human community one might ask whether genetic engineering will further widen the gap between rich and poor in our contemporary world. The push to patent genetically engineered organisms raises the basic ethical question: Is it proper to patent or claim ownership over living organisms? Will genetic engineering respect the rights of Third World people who have promoted biodiversity over thousands of years? Or will it facilitate biopiracy?

Besides the potential harmful risks that can be envisioned today, genetic engineering may also pose risks that we do not have sufficient knowledge at the moment to identify. It is after all, a very young science with many new discoveries being made in a very short space of time. It is estimated that the quantity of information in the science of genetics is doubling every two years.

Professor David Suzuki who has worked in genetics since 1961 smiles when he reflects on how the certainties that he held in the 1960s have all vanished. He writes: 'today when I tell students the hottest ideas we had in 1961 about chromosome structure and genetic regulations, they gasp and laugh in disbelief. In 1997, most of the best ideas of 1961 can be seen for what they are – wrong, irrelevant or unimportant…. So what is our hurry in biotechnology to patent ideas and rush products to market when the chances are overwhelmingly that their theoretical rationale will be wrong?'[7] Closer to home, another well-known environmentalist, David Bellamy acknowledges that 'genetically modified products worry him'.[8]

This is not an argument for stopping research in this area, but it does put a substantial burden on those who wish to engage in deliberate releases to demonstrate the safety of their products and the benefits that they will bring. Furthermore, if something does go wrong, it will be impossible to recall the organisms that are multiplying in the environment. It is not like a batch of malfunctioning cars that can be repaired and returned to the owner. Genetic engineering deals with organisms that produce, mutate and interact with other organisms in the environment.

My own position begins with the recognition that genetic engineering has the potential to reshapes other creatures in a radical ways. Furthermore, since the risks associated with it are not fully understood we should proceed with extreme caution and not release genetically modified organisms into the environment until we have addressed the ethical issues and have a much greater knowledge of the health, environmental, social and economic risks involved. We need at least a five-year moratorium on the deliberate release on genetically engineered organisms.

Before going on to deal with some of the questions it is well to remember that, while modern technology has increased the level of affluence for 20 or 30 per cent of the human family, it often comes with a sting in its tail.

The sad irony is that modern technology, especially in its chemical and nuclear phase, while it has delivered benefits to a segment of humanity in the form of better nutrition and longer life-span, has wreaked havoc on the planet. Today, its impact is so extensive and damaging that it threatens the future of many life forms, including humankind itself.

The internal combustion engine has brought increased mobility to many people in the twentieth century. Yet, the increased number of cars around the world emitting greenhouse gases threatens to destabilise the planet's climate system. A few hundred million cars being driven on good roads in different parts of the world will bring ease of mobility and comfort to many. Ten billion cars, on the other hand, could have potentially catastrophic consequences for humans and other creatures. What this means is that we need to look at the scale of our technology. This will inevitably mean that we will have to radically restructure much of our contemporary technologies for the simple reason that they are unsustainable in our finite world.

In recent times many discoveries have been found to have very adverse, unintended effects that those who developed them were unaware of. It took over two decades for scientists like Rachel Carson to discover the impact of DDT on the reproductive behaviour of birds. The widespread use of DDT as a pesticide in the US began in the 1930s. In the 1940s it was used globally, especially in malaria eradication schemes. DDT is highly persistent in the environment. By the 1950s scientists began to link DDT with the thinning of egg-shells in many species of birds and their consequent failure to reproduce. Birds of prey like the eagle, osprey and peregrine falcon were particularly affected. It was also discovered that DDT caused cancer. In 1971, after a protracted battle against chemical companies that produced DDT, it was banned in the USA. Since then it has been banned in many Northern countries, though it is still used widely in the Third World.

For almost fifty years chlorofluorocarbon (CFCs) was considered to be the perfect chemical for refrigeration. Then in the 1970s it was discovered that CFCs destroy the ozone layer of the atmosphere which protects humans and other creatures and plants from the damaging ultraviolet rays of the sun. Many of the chemical companies that manufactured CFCs denied the connection until the mid-1980s. Eugene Linden writing in *Time* magazine (10 May 1993) claims that 'in the United States those who had the power to take action engaged in self-delusion: The Reagan Administration at first dismissed the ozone threat as a non-issue, while Du Pont and other manufacturers underestimated future sales of CFCs making the hazard seem minimal'. Both industry and the regulatory agency were very much to blame.[9]

Of all the technologies which have changed the human condition and the environment in various ways none is as intrusive as genetic engineering for the simple reason that it allows humans to scramble and reprogramme the genetic code of all life forms on earth, including humans. This awesome possibility needs to be approached slowly and with great care. Commercial considerations must not be allowed to promote this technology, without a long and through public debate about the potential benefits to humankind and the earth and possible nightmares that might be created.

Genetics

Before examining the ethical issues involved in genetic engineering it might help to outline briefly, and in a very simplified way, what is involved.

Genetic engineering is a by-product of the relatively young science of genetics. The science emerged out of the pioneering work of the Austrian Augustinian, Gregory Mendel. In a paper published in 1865 he developed a theory of organic inheritance from his work on crossing garden peas that exhibited different characteristics like tallness or shortness, the presence or absence of colour in the blossoms and so on. Mendel postulated that the occurrence of visible alternative characteristics of the plants in the constant varieties and in their descendants is due to the occurrence of paired elementary units of heredity that are now called genes. Unfortunately, Mendel's work remained unrecognised for decades, until in the early 1900s various other scientists independently obtained results similar to his. When these scientists checked the biological literature they found that the experimental data on the peas and the theoretical formulation had been published by Mendel thirty years previously.

By the 1920s genetics was being used to help plant breeders improve their crops. Genetics took another leap forward in the 1950s when two young scientists, James Watson and Francis Crick, discovered the physical make up of deoxyribonucleic acid (DNA), the fundamental molecule of life. They discovered that the structure of DNA was like a double helix. The two strands were twisted around each other like a spiral staircase with bars extending across the connecting strands. These units, composed of four different chemical nucleotides, arrange themselves in an endless variety of patterns that form the genes. It is the precise ordering of the chemical base in the DNA molecule that makes each life form unique. Simple life forms like bacteria are composed of a few hundred genes. A more complex organism, like the human body, is composed of more than 100,000 genes. In the light of Watson's and Crick's discovery, biologists began to realise that by changing the ordering pattern of the genetic material they could change or modify life forms.

But this discovery, though crucial, was not sufficient to enable scientists to cut up, delete, or recombine genes. They needed tools to cut the genes and then they required a suitable mode of conveyance or vectors to insert the genetic material into another organism. The cutting tools were discovered in a group of enzymes that are called 'restriction enzymes'. They have the ability, as part of their defence mechanism, to splice up DNA. In 1973 Drs Stanley Cohen and Annie Chang inserted genes from a South African clawed toad into a bacterium – e-coli. When the e-coli reproduced themselves they also reproduced the toad gene that had been inserted into the bacterium.

Today plants and animals with genes taken from completely unrelated species are being engineered in the laboratories of biotechnology companies and released into the environment. Proponents of genetic engineering claim that it is very much in continuity with older breeding practices. As we will see later, it is nothing of the sort. Genetic engineering is a new technology. It crosses species barriers in a way that permanently alters the genetic code of living organisms.

A company called Calgene developed a genetically engineered tomato called Flavr Savr in the US and Europe. This tomato was approved by the US Food and Drug Administration (FDA) in May 1997. The goal of the experiment was to extend the shelf life of the tomato that is marketed under the brand name of 'McGregor'. Calgene invested a whopping $95 million in the process which involved isolating a gene that carries codes for an enzyme involved in the ripening process. Having discovered the enzyme the technologist blocked its expression.

As a result the tomatoes will take a few days to ripen on the vine and still maintain their firmness during shipping. As a consequences the consumer will believe that the tomato is much fresher than it is. Extending the shelf-life means that the crop can be grown much further away from the retail outlet. For example, it is now possible to grow the tomatoes in places like Central America where the labour and environmental laws are much less strict than those in the United States. Calgene has already been in touch with Mexican growers with a view to producing Flavr Savr on their lands

Scientists have also attempted to create leaner and more cost-effective pork through genetically engineered pigs even though the animals experienced extensive arthritis. They can re-engineer the genetic blueprint of an animal or plant in order to create a 'super animal' or a higher yielding plant. On the medical side, genetic engineering has created the first patented mammal, called the OncoMouse. This creature was genetically engineered with a human gene to express cancer in the mammary gland. It is now possible to create new transgenetic viruses, bacteria, plants or animals that can be used to secrete in the milk or blood large quantities of inexpensive drugs or chemicals suitable for human use. These are just a few examples of the wide range of transgenetic plants and animals that are now available.

An eco-centred moral framework

Should we, as one species among millions of others, be engaging in such experiments? I believe that our anthropocentric Western scientific values and ethical norms are not capable of addressing such issues as these in any comprehensive or effective way. Even the 'minimum ethical consensus' proposed by the theologian Hans Küng appears to be mainly human-centred. It includes the fundamental right to life (human), just treatment from the State and physical and mental integrity. The consensus is geared to creating 'the smallest possible basis for human living and acting together.[10]

How humans might relate to other species is not on this ethical landscape. Yet that relationship is a matter of life and death for many species, possibly, even the human species. Küng provides a hint at how we might attempt to construct an adequate ethical framework for contemporary problems like genetic engineering. He suggests that a global ethic be 'related to reality'. I would endorse that suggestion and attempt to broaden it by situating the human story within the large story of the earth.

In this view a satisfactory ethical framework must be based on our contemporary understanding of the relationship between humans and the rest of the natural world, not on the mechanistic world of Newton or Descartes. In the scientific world of the 1980s and 1990s the mechanistic view has been challenged by physicists and biologists. John Polkinghorne, a theologian and former professor of theoretical physics at Queen's College, Cambridge, insists that the 'world is no mere mechanism. It has a flexibility, a suppleness within its process, a freedom for the whole universe to be itself, a freedom for us to act within that universe of which we are a part'.[11] Our evolutionary history makes it very clear that humans are not disconnected from the rest of nature. Rather we are an integral part of the community of living beings and non-living reality.

Humankind evolved with other creatures during the past few million years and we are dependent on plants and animals for our survival. The well-being of the human species depends on the well-being of the whole fabric of nature. If we damage that in an irreversible way, we damage ourselves. So even from the perspective of enlightened self-interest we ought to respect the community of living beings as well as the air, water and soils of the earth to ensure our own future.

Much of the moral debate in this area concentrates on the impact of genetic engineering on human beings.[12] It focuses on whether it will benefit or damage human health. One seldom finds the more fundamental moral questions addressed: Do human beings, as one relatively young species in the community of the living, have the right to interfere in such an intrusive way by introducing exogenous DNA into the genome of another species? Genetic engineering techniques make it possible to alter in a significant way the genetic integrity of any species, be it a bacterium, plant or animal. But is it ethically right to do this particularly if the modification is harmful to the animal?

Take the case of genetically engineered salmon. A report published in 1997, commissioned by the Marine Institute of Ireland, discusses *The Nature and Current Status of Transgenetic Atlantic Salmon*. The document states that as a result of introducing growth hormone genes into a wild North Atlantic salmon the transgenetic fish grows rapidly and reaches enormous size. Studies show that within a period of fourteen months the transgenetic salmon can weigh thirty-seven times more than the ordinary salmon. These increases will probably make enormous profits for the company producing the salmon. The cost to the salmon is horrendous. In its technical and unemotive language the report notes that the experiment produces 'profound morphological abnormalities' in the progeny of the transgenetic salmon.' These included a 'disproportionate growth of the head and operculum cartilage, disimproving appearance and leading ultimately to respiratory problems'.[13] The report never raises the basic question: Do humans have the right to interfere with the genetic integrity of this species of fish?

At this very moment experiments are also being carried out on many other animals in an effort to improve livestock or develop cheap ways of producing drugs. Animal rights groups like Compassion in World Farming are rightly concerned about the suffering which genetic engineering techniques inflict on animals. Today the technology is imprecise since the expression of the gene depends on the promoters, enhancers and silencer genes. As a result all kinds of abnormalities have occurred including loss of limbs and brain defects. In many situations, because the transgenetic animal does not pass on the desired gene to its offspring, repeated experiments are necessary in order to develop the desired line for breeding purposes. In reflecting on the potential for increasing animal suffering and creating abnormal creatures Jeremy Rifkin concludes:

> The larger lesson is that the complex and multiple interactions between the inserted trangene and the chemical activity of the host animal are, for the most part, unknowable and unpredictable and can result in all sorts of novel and even bizarre pathologies in the creature.[14]

An ethical assessment of genetic engineering or cloning needs to ask the following questions: What need would justify such intervention? Would the desire to produce an animal with profitable economic traits like increased growth performance, leaner meat and greater weight justify the operation?

Viewed through an exclusively anthropocentric moral framework the answer to the may well be Yes. Charles McCarthy, an ethicist with the Kennedy Institute for Bioethics at Georgetown University in Washington D.C., writes: 'In a utilitarian context, efficiency in food production and ability to compete for world markets stand as high values which must be weighed against our recognised obligations to provide for the interests of the animals'.[15] In general the human-centred argument usually wins out, but an attempt to widen the moral universe beyond the human domain to include the rights of other species has been under way on the margins of ethical studies for a number of decades.

Eco-centred ethics

Aldo Leopold, an American ecologist, writing as far back as 1949, tried to work out an eco-centred land ethic. He insisted that no progress could be made towards shaping such an ethic until the concept of land is expanded beyond legal and economic domains. According to Leopold, looked at ecologically and ethically, land is a community which includes 'soils, waters, plants, and animals, or collectively: the land'.[16]

Leopold acknowledged that an ethic that might take such insights seriously does not preclude using land, plants or animals for human sustenance and welfare. It does, however, mean that they have a right to continue in existence in some way in their natural state. Leopold formulated his eco-centred principle as follows: 'A thing is right when it tends to preserve the integrity, stability and beauty of the biotic community. It is wrong when it tends otherwise'.[17]

Those associated with the Deep Ecology movement would go further than Leopold in framing ethical norms that regulate human interaction with the rest of nature. Their focus is often called the ecocentric or biocentric approach because they argue that ethics should be concerned about the impact of a human behaviour on ecosystems, like rivers and even on the biosphere as a whole, as in the case of global warming. For Deep ecologists ecocentrism is both an ethical imperative and also a programme for political action. They insist that 'all things in the biosphere have an equal right to live and blossom and to reach their individual forms of unfolding and self-realisation with the larger Self-Realisation'.[18]

There is no way that Deep Ecology advocates like the Norwegian philosopher Arne Naess, would countenance the kind of experiments carried out on the pigs or the salmon as described above. Deep Ecology values non-human life independently of its usefulness to human beings. It is particularly keen on promoting social and ecological policies which involve 'non-inter-ference with continuing evolution'.

Whilst I might distance myself from some positions es-poused by Deep Ecology, especially those which fail to ac-knowledge any unique place for human beings in the commu-nity of the living, I think that their insistence on the rights of other creatures and the integrity of the ecosystem as a whole must now become the context within which the ethical dimen-sion of biotechnology ought to be discussed. For example, biotechnologists are now able to eliminate the brooding instinct in turkeys blocking the gene that produces the prolactin hor-mone. Non-brooding turkeys are more productive than brood-ing birds, but is it right to engineer animals in a way that destroys their mothering instinct?

My own position is close to that of Fr Thomas Berry, an American priest who discusses ecological issues from a cosmo-logical, ethical and religious perspective. He writes that con-temporary ethics must focus its concerns on the larger commu-nity of the living. He argues that the human community is subordinate to the ecological community. The ecological im-perative is not derivative from human ethics. Human ethics is derived from the ecological imperative.

The basic ethical norm is the well-being of the comprehen-sive community, not the well-being of the human community. The earth is a single ethical system, as the universe is a single ethical system.[19] This is the first principle of an ecological ethic.

Such an ethic would demand a legal framework where the rights of the geological and biological as well as the human component or the earth community are articulated and pro-tected. Obviously the rights that we must accord to humans and the rights that we ought to grant to other creatures and entire ecosystems are not the same. The important thing is we need to begin to realize that the rest of the world is not simply there for human use or abuse.

Even moral theologians who work within the narrower moral paradigm of the Judeo-Christian tradition are beginning to insist on the intrinsic value of other creatures. Traditionally animals and plants were considered to have value merely because they are perceived to be useful to human beings, rather than because they possess intrinsic worth in themselves. Starting from the position that other creatures do have intrinsic value, Professor James A. Nash would be very sceptical about the morality of genetically engineering other creatures. He writes that since, in the Christian tradition, other species are deemed to have intrinsic value, the creation of transgenetic species should 'not be the norm but the rare exception on which the burden of proof rests. The genetic reconstruction of some species may be justified for compelling human needs in medicine, agriculture or ecological repairs (e.g. oil eating microbes), so long as it can be reasonably tested and verified that tolerable alternatives are not available, genetic diversity is not compromised and ecosystemic integrity is not endangered'.[20]

In the light of this principle it would be impossible to justify the experiment on the genetically engineered salmon and other animals that are being vigorously promoted by the biotechnology industry today. The distress caused to the animals involved and the right which animals have to preserve their own genetic integrity ought to act as a prohibition against such experiments until there is a much more extensive debate on the issue among the public. From an ethical perspective the nub of the issue revolves around whether other creatures have 'intrinsic' value. If they do, then it seems logical to argue that they have rights that their own 'specialness' especially the species boundary be respected by another creature. If they do not and are merely objects, then, of course, there is no ethical imperative to respect their species uniqueness. Humans can exploit them for any purpose whatever. In the present global commercial climate such exploitation will be driven by what is considered useful, profitable and acceptable for humans.

Following on from an ecocentred approach one can then assess the impact of an activity on humans and the environment. The question is: Does genetic engineering pose such a threat to human health and the environment that the deliberate release of genetically engineered organisms should not be allowed at this point in time?

Risks to human health and the environment

The dangers which are posed by the development of biotechnological products are real. At a meeting in Asilomar in 1975 a group of scientists drawn from the Committee on Recombinant DNA of the US National Academy of Sciences, which included the Nobel Prize winner, James Watson, warned about the dangers of genetic engineering. They stated that 'there is serious concern that some of these artificially recombinant DNA molecules could prove biologically hazardous'.[21] This conference upheld the moratorium on recombinant DNA experiments. Jeremy Rifkins accepts that the reason for the moratorium had more to do with the potential legal liabilities of creating bio-hazards than concern for human health or the environmental risks of the new technology.[22]

Almost twenty years later an international group of scientists meeting in Malaysia in July 1994 called attention to the scientific flaws inherent in the genetic engineering paradigm. The believe that genetic engineering is based on the false premise that each individual feature of an organism is encoded in one or more specific, stable gene and that the transfer of these genes results in the transfer of these discrete features. The truth is that no gene works in isolation but as part of an extremely complex genetic network. In fact the function of each gene are dependent on the context of all the other genes in the genome. The same gene, for example, will have very different effects from individual to individual, because other genes are different.

The scientists who met in Malaysia pointed out that the development of any trait results from many complex interactions between genes and their cellular context and the external environment. Numerous layers of feedback mechanisms link all these levels. These scientists insist that, in a significant number of cases, it is impossible to predict the consequences of transferring a gene from one type of organism to another. Furthermore, genetically engineered organisms, especially micro-organisms, may migrate, mutate and be transferred to other organisms and species. In some cases the stability of affected organisms and ecosystems could be affected and threatened.[23]

It is for this reason that Dr Mae-Wan Ho, a geneticist opposed to genetic engineering, argues that genetic engineering is a crude and imprecise operation and, consequently, is inherently hazardous to health and biodiversity. The insertion of a foreign gene into the host genome is a random process, not under the control of the genetic engineer. The horizontal gene transfer is achieved through the use of artificial vectors. The transferred gene can give rise to random genetic effects including cancer.[24] She believes that the technology will contribute to an increase in the frequency of horizontal transfer of those genes that are responsible for virulence and antibiotic resistance, and allow them to recombine to generate new pathogens.[25]

Such fears are dismissed by other geneticists. But even if there is a remote chance of these problems occurring the whole genetic engineering enterprise should be put on hold until independent scientific research has addressed these issue over a considerable period of time.

Potential risks to humans and the environment

Some of the risks to human health and the environment include: the potential to cause allergies; an increase in antibiotic resistance and toxicity; the consumer being misled into thinking that produce is fresh and, finally, unpredictable gene expression in the engineered organism. Because of these risks a group of scientists in the United States, calling themselves the Council for Responsible Genetics, have called for a more proactive approach from the regulatory agency – the Food and Drug Administration (FDA) – in monitoring and regulating genetically engineered foods.

It is well-known that allergies in humans are caused by particular proteins. Genetic engineering involves adding new proteins to altered products. The FDA warns that new proteins in foods might cause allergic reactions in some people. Transgenic crops could bring new allergens into foods that sensitive individuals would not be in a position to avoid. It is possible, for example, to transfer the gene for one of the many allergenic proteins found in milk into vegetables like carrots. People who ought to avoid milk would not be aware that transgenic carrots contained milk proteins.

It is important to emphasise that this problem is unique to genetic engineering. Genetic engineering routinely moves proteins into the food supply from organisms that have never been consumed as food by human beings. Some of those proteins could be food allergens, since virtually all known food allergens are proteins. The public should be alert to the possibility of an increase in allergenicity as a result of genetic engineering. A study by scientists at the University of Nebraska found that soya beans genetically engineered to contain Brazil-nut proteins caused reactions in individuals allergic to Brazil-nuts. Blood serum from people known to be allergic to Brazil-nuts was tested for the appropriate antibody response to the gene transferred to the soya bean. When seven out of nine volunteers responded to the genetically engineered soya bean the researchers concluded that the allergenicity had been transferred with the transferred gene.

Scientists have a limited ability to predict whether a particular protein will be a food allergen, if consumed by humans. The only sure way to determine whether a protein will be an allergen is through experience. Thus importing proteins, particularly from non-food sources, is always involves a risk of allergenicity. It is generally recognized that there has been a significant rise in allergies, especially among children, in recent decades. With 8 percent of children showing allergic reactions to many commonly eaten foods it seems foolish in the extreme to do anything that might increase allergenicity. It is also worth bearing in mind that many of the genes being transferred to the trangenetic food have never been part of the human diet since the beginning of human evolution over two million years ago.

Genetic engineering often uses genes for antibiotic resistance as 'selectable markers'. Early in the engineering process, these markers help select cells that have taken up the foreign genes. Although they have no further use, the genes continue to be expressed in plant tissues. Most genetically engineered plant foods carry fully functioning antibiotic resistant genes. The most commonly used marker genes are the npt11 gene that confers resistance to kanamycin, neomycin and geneticin and the bla gene that confers resistance to ampicillin.

The presence of antibiotic resistant genes in foods could have two harmful effects. First, eating these foods could reduce the effectiveness of antibiotics that are taken with such a meal. Antibiotic resistance genes produce enzymes that can degrade antibiotics. If a tomato with an antibiotic resistant gene is eaten at the same time as an antibiotic, it could destroy the antibiotic in the stomach.

Secondly, the resistant genes could be transferred to human or animal pathogens, making them impervious to antibiotics. If transfer were to occur, it could aggravate the already serious health problem of antibiotic-resistant disease organisms. Although unmediated transfers of genetic material from plants to bacteria is highly unlikely, even a slight risk of this happening ought to require careful scrutiny in light of the seriousness of antibiotic resistance in the population at large. The discovery by scientists at Cologne University in 1998 that DNA which had been fed to a mouse survived in the digestive system and subsequently invaded other cells in the mouse's body should raise serious questions and should slow down the entry of genetically engineered products into the food chain until there is much more research on their ultimate impact on human health.[26]

It is also true that the highly mosaic character of most vector constructs makes them structurally unstable and prone to recombination. According to scientists opposed to genetic engineering this may be why viral-resistant transgenic plants generate recombinant viruses more readily than non-trangenetic plants.[27]

Many organisms have the ability to produce toxic substances. These substances help the organism defend itself against many predators in their environment. In some cases, plants contain inactive pathways leading to toxic substances. The addition of new genetic material, through genetic engineering, could reactivate these inactive pathways. Alternatively it could increase the levels of toxic substances within the plants. This could happen, for example, if the on/off signals associated with the introduced gene were located on the genome in places where they could turn on the previously inactive genes. In the light of these considerations many argue that genetically engineered foods pose new and unique challenges to food safety.

Some of the new genes being added to crops can remove heavy metals like mercury from the soil and concentrate them in the plant tissue. The purpose of creating such crops is to make possible the use of municipal sludge as fertiliser. Sludge contains useful plant nutrients, but often cannot be used as fertiliser because it is contaminated with toxic heavy metals. The idea is to engineer plants to remove and sequester those metals in inedible parts of plants. In a tomato, for example, the metals would be concentrated in the roots; in potatoes in the leaves. Turning on the genes in only some parts of the plants requires the use of genetic on/off switches that turn on only in specific tissues, like leaves.

Such products pose risks of contaminating foods with high levels of toxic metals if the on/off switches are not completely turned off in edible tissues. There are also environmental risks associated with the handling and disposal of the metal-contaminated parts of plants after harvesting. This is a classic example of a technological fix for an environmental problem that ought to be addressed at its source. The way to guarantee that sewage sludge can be used in agriculture is to ensure that toxic substances do not enter sewerage plants in the first instance.

Generally when people focus on health hazards associated with genetic engineering they concentrate on the genetic material that is added to organisms. There is also the possibility that the removal of genes can cause problems. For example, genetic engineering might be used to produce decaffeinated coffee beans by deleting or turning off genes associated with the production of caffeine. But caffeine helps protect coffee beans against fungi. Beans that are unable to produce caffeine might be coated with fungi, which can produce toxins. Fungal toxins, such as aflatoxin, are potent human toxins that can remain active through processes of food preparation. Finally it is worth noting that the Food and Drug Administration (FDA) is concerned that toxins may be produced at unusually high levels as a result of genetic engineering.

A possible consequence of genetically engineered foods is an alteration of the nutritional content of the resulting product. The FDA cautions that nutritional value could be significantly decreased without the crop exhibiting any outward signs. Humans have come to rely on certain characteristics of fruits and vegetables to indicate nutritional quality and flavour. For example, bright colour in peppers, apples and other fruits is generally associated with taste and ripeness. Genetic engineering may mislead consumers into buying fruits and vegetables which appear to be fresh and just about ripe, but in fact are engineered to last longer on the shelf and as a consequence may lack nutritional quality. This would have serious implications for public health and needs to be taken on board by monitoring and regulatory agencies.

Potential future problems

History has shown that it takes a few decades for the full set of risks associated with any technology to be identified. In the 1920s no one predicted that CFCs could cause such harm to the ozone layer. The ability to imagine what might go wrong with genetic engineering is limited by the current knowledge in such disciplines as physiology, genetics, and nutrition.

We should not forget too quickly how pressures from the food industry and government agencies led to the failure of the UK authorities to link BSE with a new variant of the incurable human condition CJD. Those who raised questions about this connection in the mid-1980s were often criticised and even ridiculed by their colleagues. Dr Tim Holt, a Yorkshire doctor, told a UK government enquiry into BSE how a pathologist at the Government's central veterinary laboratory investigating mad cow disease said that the transmission to humans was as 'unlikely as a being struck by lightening'.[28] Finally, with other faulty technology mistakes can be rectified by redesigning the machinery, mistakes in the area of genetic engineering are much more difficult to correct.

The need for caution is highlighted by the controversy surrounding the production of transgenetic pigs to provide organs for human transplant operations. Companies on both sides of the Atlantic have engineered pigs to carry human protein on the surface of their cells so that the organs will not be rejected by the human immune system. At first glance this seems to be a practical way of meeting the demand for organs for transplant operations. Unfortunately, researchers have found that the pigs can carry at least two retroviruses. One of these has the potential to infect human cells. Even though the US Food and Drug Administration (FDA) have been provided with the results of the research they have continued to allow the transplants to take place. One of the researchers involved felt that the least the FDA should have done is ban the transplants.[29] Given the presence of these viruses many scientists would argue that pig organs can never be a safe replacement for human lives.[30]

Environmental concerns
Genes form a holistic system, with one gene affecting multiple traits and multiple genes affecting one trait. Consequently, scientists cannot always predict how a single gene will be expressed in a new system. For example, splicing a gene for human growth hormones into mice produces very large mice; splicing the same gene into pigs produces skinny, cross-eyed, arthritic animals. The FDA warns that splicing a single gene into an organism for a single desired effect may unintentionally cause other harmful reactions within that organism which are not detectable.

Organisms engineered to grow under adverse conditions run the risk of becoming weeds either directly or by breeding with wild relatives. Here, weeds means all plants which are found in places where humans do not want to have them growing. In each case, the plants are found growing unaided and have unwanted effects as far as the farmer is concerned. If genetically engineered plants became weeds this could damage large tracks of agricultural lands, severely limit crop yields and cause immeasurable destruction to sensitive ecosystems.

Some weeds result from the accidental introduction of alien plants, but many are the result of organisms introduced for agricultural and horticultural purposes. Johnson grass that was intentionally introduced into the United States has become a serious weed. In Britain serious damage is being caused by escaped mink that have no natural predator in that environment. In the Galapagos Islands feral cats have wrecked havoc on the defenceless island fauna. In Africa the South American Water Hyacinth has choked freshwater habitats. A new combination of traits, produced as a result of genetic engineering, might enable crops to thrive in an environment in which they would then be considered a weed. For example a rice plant engineered to be salt-tolerant if it escaped into a marine estuaries could cause enormous damage. The possibility that this will happen increases as more and more genetically engineered organisms are released into the environment.

Biotech scientists and regulators often dismiss the possibility of genetically engineered crops becoming super weeds because they argue that most staple crops have been so weakened genetically by the domestication process that the addition of an engineered trait will not enhance their competitiveness. While this might be true of crops like corn, many crops like alfalfa, barley, potatoes, wheat, sorghum, broccoli, cabbage and radishes do retain their weedy traits. For example, a gene changing the oil-composition of a crop might move into nearby weedy relatives in which the new oil composition would enable the seeds to survive the winter. The ability to survive winter cold might allow the plant to become a weed or might intensify the weedy properties it already possessed. This is why Dr Margaret Mellon, a molecular biologist, and Dr Jane Rissler, a plant pathologist, both of whom work with the Union of Concerned Scientists in the US, argue that the 'possibility that engineering will convert crops into new weeds is a major risk of genetic engineering'.[31]

Even more serious is the danger of what is called 'gene flow'. This refers to the possibility of transferring a gene from a transgenetic plant to a weedy relative by way of cross-pollination. Novel genes placed in crops will not necessarily stay in the fields in which they are planted. If relatives of the altered crops are growing near the field, the new gene can easily move, via pollen, into those plants. The new traits might confer on to the wild or weedy relatives of crop plants the ability to thrive in unwanted places, making them weeds as defined above. If a herbicide-resistant gene jumped to a wild weedy relative then that plant might become resistant to the particular herbicide. This form of genetic pollution could easily become a major nuisance to farmers worldwide.

Many fear that the planing of genetically engineered oil seed rape in Europe in 1999 will mean that 'herbicide-tolerant rape will undoubtedly become part of the established volunteer weed populations that occur in many cereal rotations'.[32] The infestation may occur even where farmers do not grow the GE oil seed rape themselves. It can happen that a GE oil seed rape grown in an adjacent field can pollinate plants in a neighbouring field and produce seeds that are herbicide-tolerant.

Mistakes can also happen as the following two examples demonstrate. In the late 1980s a company called Biotechnica

International genetically engineered a micro-organism (Brady-rhizobium japonica) to improve nitrogen fixation in plants. The company contracted the Louisiana Agricultural Experiment Station to conduct field trials for one year by planting soya beans coated with the genetically engineered rhizobia. After the experiment the plants and seeds were incinerated, the fields were reploughed and replanted and Biotechnica ceased to have anything to do with the field trials. However, subsequent trials on that land revealed that the genetically engineered rhyzobia were out-competing the indigenous strain. This was not expected to happen. The act of reploughing the area, rather than helping, in fact spread the genetically engineered rhyzobia over a four-acre plot. The case illustrates the unpredictability of genetically engineered experiments. According to one scientist: 'One of the major considerations about this case is that a microbe for which there existed an extensive historical database was used in a well-planned and thoroughly reviewed experiment, and an unpredictable result was still obtained'.[33]

A genetically engineered bacterium (Klebsiella) was found to produce dramatic changes in the soil food web and therefore inhibit plant growth. The bacterium was engineered to produce ethanol from agricultural waste as a way of generating fuel. But when added to the soil it was found that it produced a significant decrease in growth in both roots and the shoots of wheat. There was also a decrease in beneficial soil fungi, an increase in parasitic nematodes and bacteria. Stopping the spread of such a bacterium, once released, will be very difficult.[34]

A second major environmental concern is the increased use of herbicides. Over half of the crops currently under development are being engineered for herbicide resistance, permitting increased use of these harmful chemicals. The permission granted in 1998 by the Environmental Protection Agency in Ireland to Monsanto Ireland Ltd, to conduct field trials of sugar beet that has been genetically engineered to be resistant to the herbicide RoundUp, raised questions about the nature of these herbicides and their increased use.

The company claims that even after long-term application there is no effect on the environment. RoundUp is marketed as an environmentally-friendly herbicide. Monsanto also claims that the use of RoundUp-ready seeds will lead to a decrease in the use of herbicides. Such claims need to be thoroughly scrutinised. RoundUp is a broad spectrum non-selective herbicide which kills all plants, including grasses, broadleaf plants and woody plants. The active agent in RoundUp, glyphosate, is an organophosphate. Unlike other organophosphates it does not affect the nervous system of animals. But that does not make it environmentally friendly.

Critics of Monsanto point out that it is very difficult to measure glyphosate residue in the environment. Only a few laboratories have the sophisticated equipment and expertise necessary. This means that data are often lacking on residue levels in food and in the environment and existing data may not be fully reliable.

While the acute toxicity of glyphosate for mammals is very low, it can interfere with some enzyme functions in animals. In California glyphosate is the third most commonly reported cause of pesticide-related illness among agricultural workers. Glyphosate causes damage to the environment. Many species of wild plants are damaged or killed by applications of less than 10 micrograms per plant. These plants are particularly vulnerable when it is spread from the air. Fish and invertebrates are also very sensitive to formulations of glyphosate as are beneficial insects like lacewings and ladybugs.

More recent studies have shown that the problems with RoundUp stem not so much from the glyphosate but rather from the unlabelled 'inert' ingredients that aim to make the herbicide more efficient. According to Joseph Mendelson, 'RoundUp consists of 99.04 per cent "inert" ingredients, many of which have been identified, including polyethoxylated tallowamine surfactant (known as POEA), related organic acids of flyphosate, isopropylamine, and water. Researchers have found that the acute lethal dose of POEA is less than one-third that of glyphosate alone. Studies by Japanese researchers on poisoning victims discovered that this "inert" ingredient caused acute toxicity in patients.[35]

There is also evidence that plants that are grown in the presence of weed-killers can suffer from stress. They react by producing or failing to produce certain proteins or substances. Members of the bean family produce higher levels of plant-oestrogens (phyto-oestogens) when grown in the presence of glyphosate. Excessive levels of these oestrogens present a risk to children. These plant-oestrogens mimic the role of hormones in the human body. They can be particularly disruptive of the human reproductive system, especially for young males.[36]

There is also good reason to be sceptical about claims that genetically engineered plants will lead to fewer chemicals in agriculture. In soybean cultivation Monsanto maintained, in documents prepared for the US authorities, that it now takes between one and five applications of different herbicides to control weeds. With RoundUp only one or, possibly, two applications will be needed. Yet in their advice to farmers in Argentina, Monsanto recommended that RoundUp be used with RoundUp Ready soybeans before sowing, when the plants are young, after three or four leaves have appeared and whenever the farmer finds weeds. This is quite a different scenario.[37]

Something similar has happened with AgrEvo's genetically engineered oil seed rape that is resistant to the herbicide glufosinate which is destined to be planted in Europe in 1999. The company has increased the production facilities for glufosinate in the US and Germany and expects sales to increase in the next five to seven years. In fact it is alleged that the reason that AgrEvo has entered into the GE market is to boost its herbicide sales.[38]

In January 1997 Monsanto agreed to change its advertising for glyphosate-based products, including RoundUp, in response to complaints by the New York Attorney General's office that the ads were misleading. As part of the agreement, Monsanto will not use the term 'biodegradable' or 'environmentally friendly' in its advertisements for glyphosate-based products in New York State. They also agreed to pay $50,000 towards the State's cost for pursuing the case. Monsanto claims it did not violate any federal, state or local law and that its claims were 'true and not misleading in any way'. The company states that it entered into the agreement for settlement purposes only in order to avoid costly litigation.[39] In November 1997 the Dutch Advertisement Code Committee (ACC) found that Monsanto's advertisements for RoundUp were misleading. The ACC judged that Monsanto's herbicide is not biologically degradable and that their ECO claim is in conflict with the truth.

Companies like Monsanto claim that by producing crops that are resistant to herbicide they will reduce the amount of harmful chemicals entering the environment. They fail to inform the public that it is also a very cost-effective operation for the company. At present it costs between $40 and $100 million to bring a new pesticide through the regulatory process to the farmers' fields. It only takes $1 million to develop a new plant variety. Pat Mooney believes that 'economics dictate that chemical companies invent new crop varieties adaptable to the company's chemicals rather than adapt expensive pesticides to the inexpensive seeds'.[40]

Genetic engineering also threatens biodiversity. The UK Advisory Committee on Releases to the Environment is concerned that when crops which are genetically engineered to be resistant to herbicides become common they will have a devastating impact on wildlife. Fields of genetically engineered crops could lead to starvation for birds and insects that depend on these seeds as a source of food. The committee's chairman, John Beringer, Professor of Molecular Genetics at Bristol University, said that 'It could be cranking up the pressure on species if this technology proceeds to the limits'.[41]

Many insects contain genes that render them susceptible to pesticides. Often these susceptible genes predominate in natural populations of insects. These genes are a valuable natural resource because they allow pesticides to remain as effective pest-control tools. The more benign the pesticide, the more valuable the genes that make pests susceptible to it.

Certain genetically engineered crops threaten the continued susceptibility of pests to one of nature's most valuable pesticides: the Bacillus thuringiensis or Bt toxin. These Bt crops are genetically engineered to contain a gene for the Bt toxin. Because the crops produce the toxin in most plant tissues throughout the life cycle of the plant, pests are constantly exposed to it. This continuous exposure in time will render the Bt pesticide useless, unless specific measures are instituted to avoid the development of such resistance. In fact in both laboratory and field situations a number of species, including the Colorado potato beetle, have developed a resistance to the Bt toxin. In 1996 Monsanto's Nu Corn which contained the Bt toxin failed to preform as expected due to hot weather and drought conditions. Even in field tests the genetically engineered gene killed only 80 percent of the bollworms that attack cotton. The fact that 20 percent survived means that a 'super bug', resistent to Bt, will almost inevitably emerge.

On the larger stage Vandana Shiva, an Indian scientist who studies biodiversity, claims that genetically engineering, even now, is working against crop diversity and is narrowing the genetic base of agriculture to only a few crops. In 1998 two commercially staple crops were being genetically engineered – soya and maize. In place of hundreds of legumes and beans eaten around the world there was only one GE soya. In the places of different varieties of cereals – millets, wheat and rice – there is only maize. She goes on to point out that genetically engineered crops are based on expanding monocultures of the same variety evolved for a single function. As the biotechnology industry takes root in different countries this monoculture tendency will continue, further undermining agricultural biodiversity and, thereby creating ecological vulnerability.

The addition of foreign genes to plants could also have serious consequences for wildlife in a number of circumstances. For example, engineering crop plants, such as tobacco or rice, to produce plastics or pharmaceuticals could endanger mice or deer who consume crop debris left in the fields after harvesting. Fish that have been engineered to contain metal-sequestering proteins (such fish have been suggested as living pollution clean-up devices) could be harmful if consumed by other fish or racoons.

One of the most common applications of genetic engineering is the production of virus-tolerant crops. Such crops are produced by engineering components of viruses into the plant genomes. For reasons not well understood, plants producing viral components on their own are resistant to subsequent infection by those viruses. Such plants, however, pose other risks of creating new or worse viruses through recombination.

Recombination can occur between the plant-produced viral genes and closely related genes of incoming viruses. Such recombination may produce viruses that can infect a wider range of hosts or that may be more virulent than the parent viruses.

In the late 1980s the National Institute of Allergy in the US sought an animal model suitable for studying AIDS. Researchers introduced the AIDS virus into mice. Critics of the experiment feared that if the AIDS-infected mice escaped this could create a new and even more deadly source of AIDS infection. Those conducting the experiment dismissed such fears as unfounded and alarmist. A study conducted by Dr Robert Gallo, one of the co-discoverers of the AIDS virus, and subsequently published in the magazine *Science*, cautioned against using animal research models. He and his colleagues argued that the AIDS virus carried by the experimental mice might combine with other viruses that are carried by mice. This could result in the creation of a new more virulent form of AIDS that could be transmitted in novel ways, even through the air.[42]

Genetically engineered crops could devastate Third World agriculture

On the social level there is the concern that genetically engineered crops will displace crops grown naturally by farmers in Third World countries and in the process disrupt the lives of millions of poor people. In the US two biotechnology companies have produced vanilla from plant cell cultures in laboratories. The price of naturally produced vanilla is about $1,200 per pound. The biotechnology companies estimate that they can commercially produce genetically engineered vanilla for about £25 per pound. Such a development would wipe out the livelihood of about 100,000 farmers in Third World countries. 70,000 alone live in Madagascar.

Developments like these could constitute a economic disaster for many Southern countries where biodiversity is already under severe strain. Similar research is under way to genetically engineer other crops that are crucial to Third World economies. These include coffee, tobacco, cocoa, coconut, palm oil, sugar and ginseng. Genetically engineered varieties may thrive in temperate zones and thus ravage many Third World economies that are dependent on one or other of these commodities. These countries have no fall-back industries capable of absorbing their redundant farmers. From my many years in the Philippines I know that the lives of millions of copra farmers would be devastated if coconuts oil was produced in temperate zones.

Third World people are aware of the potential damage that genetically engineered organisms could do to their society and environment. Fifty peasant, indigenous and environmental groups from all over Latin America gathered in Quito, Equador, in January 1999 to review developments in agricultural biotechnology. They published a Latin American Declaration on Transgenic Organisms. The document rejects genetic engineering 'because it is an ethically questionable technology which violates the integrity of human life, of species which have inhabited our planet for millions of years'. The document also focuses on the economic and social impact of genetic engineering.

Genetic engineering is a technology driven by commercial interest. It is not necessary. It forces us to become dependent on the TNCs which control it, putting our autonomy to decisions about productions systems and food security into real danger. Especially in the field of agriculture, there are traditional and alternative technologies which do not pose such risks and which are compatible with the conservation of biodiversity.

In India environmentalists, farmers and peasant groups have protested against the permission, given by the Indian Government to Monsanto, to field-test genetically engineered cotton seeds. In the Southern Indian States of Karnataka and Andhra Pradesh farmers have begun to burn such fields. The campaign against genetically engineered crops has been labelled 'Cremation Monsanto'. One of the main criticisms by the group is that Monsanto have not taken the biosafety measures they would be forced to take in trials in First World countries. They claim, for example, that there are no buffer zone between the test fields and the rest of the farm lands. Locals claim that in Europe the company would not be able to get away with such a policy.[43]

In reality biotech companies do not always keep the rules when conducting trials in First World countries. In February 1999 Monsanto were fined £17,000 for failing to observe the six-feet buffer zone at a test site in Lincolnshire where GE oil seed rape was been grown. It also appeared that funding for monitoring was grossly inadequate. A mere £80,000 was allocated to monitor the 340 test sites in Britain during 1998. As a result only 70 sites were visited.[44]

Some of the agribusiness companies promote their technology by talking about transferring the technology to the South. To date there has been very little transfer of genetic engineering technology from the transnational corporations to Third World countries. In fact as we will see later when discussing the 'terminator' gene, Northern companies are doing everything possible to avoid any such transfer of technology. The World Bank Panel on Transgenic Crops concluded that technology transfer between transnational corporations and less developed countries were so rare that the examples they cited were exceptional.[45]

As with human health risks, it is unlikely that all the potential risks to the environment have been identified. At this point, biology and ecology are too poorly understood to be certain that scientists can comprehensively rule out any major and irreversible damage to the environment. Therefore we ought to proceed with extreme caution. This point was made forcibly by Robin Grove-White, Director of the Study of Environmental Change,

Lancaster University, in a letter to *The Independent* (14 June 1998) in the wake of Prince Charles's article on genetic engineering which appeared in *The Daily Telegraph* (8 June 1998) the previous week. Mr Grove-White wrote:

> Last year, in a study sponsored, to its credit, by Unilever (itself a potential beneficiary of the technology), we found that the panoply of ministerial advisory committees and other regulatory mechanisms is failing utterly to engage with issues of central significance to most people- particularly, the unknowns surrounding future cumulative dependency on genetically engineered crops and foods, with the risks of unforeseen (because unforeseeable in terms of current scientific understanding) synergies and ecological or public health mishaps.

Will biotech agriculture feed the world?

Given the huge financial stakes involved it is understandably that all the stops are being pulled out in this battle for control of food production. The biotechnology industry has retained the services of a global PR company Burston Marsteller. This company specialises in crisis management and handling difficult or unsavoury situations. For example it advised Babcock and Wilcox, the builders of the Three Mile Island nuclear installation in the US, during the crisis in 1979. It also helped Union Carbide manage publicity in the aftermath of the Bhopal tragedy which killed over 1,500 in India. Among its clients, in recent times where the repressive regimes in Indonesia, Argentina and South Korea.

In a document leaked to the media in August 1997 Burston Marsteller advised the biotech companies 'that they cannot hope to win the arguments over the risks posed by genetically modified food, including the environmental dangers' (*The Guardian*, 6 August 1997). The biotech companies were advised to focus on 'symbols', not logic'. These symbols ought to elicit 'hope, satisfaction, caring and self-esteem'.

The biotechnology industry promotes itself by pointing to the benefits it will bring to human beings in food production and health care. Biotech companies like Monsanto claim that one of the main reasons they for opted genetically engineered crops is that they are convinced that GE food will be needed to feed a growing world population. Monsanto's chief executive, Robert Shapiro, developed this theme in a long interview with Joan Magretta in the *Harvard Business Review*, January-February 1997.[46] He argued that genetic engineering of food crops is a further improvement on the Green Revolution that saved Asia from starvation in the 1960s and 1970s. Similar arguments have been put forward by scientists, including Professor Christopher Leaver, professor of plant sciences at the University of Oxford. He points to the harsh realities of global population increase and shrinking agricultural lands. He claims that the only way to feed this growing population is through the use of gene technology. He also believes that it will be more environmentally friendly as it will involve the use of fewer chemicals in agriculture.[47]

Critics of genetic engineering reject the argument that GE foods will stave off global famine. They also question the accepted wisdom that the impact of the Green Revolution has been entirely positive. Dr Vandana Shiva in correspondence with Norman Borlaug, considered by many to be the father of the Green Revolution, debunks many of the myths surrounding the Green Revolution. Dr Shiva challenges the first myth that India was unable to feed itself until the Green Revolution was launched. She points out that the last famine in India took place in 1942 during British rule. She admits that India experienced a severe drought in 1966 and was forced to import 10,000 tons of grain from the US. She indicts the US administration who 'exploited this scarcity in its use of food as a weapon and forced non-sustainable, resource-inefficient, capital and chemical-intensive agriculture on one of the most ancient agricultural civilisations in the world. American agricultural experts like Borlaug did not introduce the Green Revolution to "buy time" for India. They introduced it to sell chemicals to India'.[48]

The same 'feed the world' arguments are being recycled by the promoters of genetic engineering today. In reality famine and hunger around the world have more to do with the absence of land reform, social inequality, biases against women in many cultures, lack of access to cheap credit and basic technologies, than a lack of agribusiness super seeds.

This fact was recognized by the participants who attended the World Food Summit in Rome in November 1996. They acknowledged that main causes of hunger are economic and social. People are hungry because they do not have access to food production processes or the money to buy food. Those who wish to banish hunger should address those social and economic inequalities that create poverty and not pretend that a 'magic' technology will solve all the problems.

My experience confirms this approach. I lived in Mindanao during the El Nino induced drought of 1983. There was a severe food shortages among the tribal people in the highlands. The drought destroyed their cereal crops and they could no longer get food in the tropical forest which had been logged out during the previous decades. Even during the height of the drought agribusiness corporations were exporting tropical fruit from the lowlands. There was also sufficient rice and corn in the lowlands but the tribal people did not have the money to buy it. Had it not been for food-aid from non-governmental organisations many would have starved.

Returning to Professor Leaver's article in *The Guardian*, I find it interesting that he is silent about the economic and social factors, like land ownership, that give rise to poverty and mal-nutrition. He confines his suggestions to hi-tech solutions, which in my experience usually benefit the better-off farmers. Does he think that agribusiness companies will distribute ge-netically engineered food free to the hungry poor who have no money? Are land reform and economic policies aimed at help-ing small, subsistence farmers, no longer important? Is he not worried that genetic engineering will give enormous control of the staple foods of the world to a handful of Northern agri-business companies? Most other people consider these compa-nies to be dedicated, first and foremost, to making profits.

It is also worth remembering that the Green Revolution has contributed to the 'loss of three-quarters of the genetic diversity of major food crops and that the rate of erosion continues at close to 2 per cent per annum'.[49] No wonder plant geneticists accuse plant breeders of building the roof with stones taken from the foundations. Eroding genetic diversity will be exacer-bated by the widespread introduction of genetically engineered crops.

Terminator gene

The development by a Monsanto-owned company of what is benignly called a Technology Protection System, but what is more aptly called terminator technology, is another reason for asserting that the feed-the-world argument is completely spu-rious. This technology, if it becomes widespread, will surely strike the death knell for the 1.4 billion small, subsistence farmers who live mainly in the Third World. Sharing seeds among farmers has been at the very heart of subsistence farm-ing since the domestication of staple food crops eleven thou-sand years ago. The terminator technology would effectively stop farmers sharing seeds. Hope Shand, research director with the Canadian RAFI group is alarmed at such a development:

'Half the world's farmers are poor. They provide food for more than a billion people but they can't afford to buy seeds every growing season. Seed collection is vital for them'.[50] Terminator technology will enable Monsanto to control and profit from farmers from every corner of the globe. It will lock farmers into a regime of buying genetically engineered seeds that are herbicide-tolerant and insect-resistant, copperfastening them on to the chemical threadmill.

For poor farmers in Third World countries, and the communities who depend on the food they produce, the widespread dissemination of food from terminator seeds will mean hunger, starvation and death. It is worth noting that the farmers of the South are the target market for terminator seeds. Delta and Pine has specifically suggested that rice and wheat farmers in countries like India, China and Pakistan are a priority market.

At an ethical level I suggest that a technology that, in the words of Professor Richard Lewontin of Harvard University, 'introduces a "killer" transgene that prevents the germ of the harvested grain from developing' must be considered grossly immoral.[51] Furthermore, if anything goes wrong the terminator genes could spread to neighbouring crops and wild and weedy relatives of the plant that has been engineered to commit suicide. This would jeopardize the food security of many poor people. No wonder that there are those who consider it a form of biological warfare on subsistence farmers.

The ethics of patenting life forms

One of the most problematic areas for genetic engineering from an ethical perspective revolves around the whole area of patenting. Even if one is not persuaded by the eco-centred ethical argument that other species have a right to their genetic integrity, or discounts the risks to human health and the environment posed by genetically engineered products there are good ethical reasons for opposing the patenting of living organisms. The process of patenting living organisms which began in the US and is now in place in Europe and Japan will remove living creatures from the domain of the commons where they have served humans and other creatures and transform them into the private property of a handful of Northern Transnational Corporations (TNCs).

Life, which was until now considered sacred and a gift from the divine in almost all the religions and cultures of the world, is now portrayed in the patenting era as a human invention. Rather than being appreciated in a holistic way, living organisms are now seen primarily as collections of genes and chemicals that can be engineered in a variety of ways and, subsequently, bought and sold by the patent holder.

With patenting, human beings claim to have invented plants and animals and therefore to have exclusive control over them. If the scramble to patent living forms gathers pace this will undoubtedly devalue the meaning of life across the global society. No part of the earth will be sacred in the future. Besides it could well mean that within a few short years 'the entire human genome ... would be owned by a handful of companies and governments'.[52]

Biopiracy

The patenting of Third World genetic resources by First World corporations or institutions is a form of theft. It involves appropriating the biological resources of poor, vulnerable Third World communities by rich, politically powerful corporations. Much of the raw material used in genetically engineered food and medicinal plants is found in Third World countries. In recent years biotechnology companies have been collecting this material, patenting their products and in the process making huge profits. Even before the advent of recombinant DNA technology Eli Lily was in a position to make millions of dollars by developing a drug to treat some cancers from a plant called the rosy periwinkle which is found in the rainforest of Madagascar. In 1993 alone the company made $160 million profit in sales but did not contribute one dollar to Madagascar where the plant was found.

Patenting will intensify and exacerbate the plunder of the Third World's natural resources. Microorganisms, plants, animals and even the genes of indigenous people have been patented for the production of pharmaceuticals and other products. It cannot be just to design international mechanisms that force developing nations to pay royalties to the wealthy industrial nations for products derived from their own natural resources.

Most of the world's germplasm for crops and animals is held in seed banks either in the North or controlled by the North, though it originated in the South. To appropriate this, through patenting legislation, constitutes a new form of colonialism. This time it is not merely the gold, silver or labour of poor people that is being colonised, but living beings in their community. Biotech scouts have used the knowledge of indigenous plants, which local people have accumulated over centuries, in their search for plants and animals which may have an agricultural or medical use and then patented these products.

The immorality of such behaviour is magnified further when one considers the simple fact that the species and genetic diversity is available today because countless generations of Third World farmers protected, preserved, propagated and shared these species freely with others. Vandana Shiva points out:

> The common pool of knowledge has contributed immeasurably to the vast agricultural and medicinal plant diversity that exists today. Thus, the concept of individual "property"

rights to either the resource or to the knowledge remain alien to the local community. This undoubtedly exacerbates the usurpation of the knowledge of indigenous people with serious consequences for them and for biodiversity conservation.[53]

Now all this richness is destined to be privatised for the exclusive benefit of Northern corporations .

The neem tree

Two examples drawn from India and West Africa illustrate what is now happening. The neem tree is found all over India. Farmers and traditional healers have used this tree for a variety of purposes for hundreds of years. In ancient Sanskrit texts the tree is called *sarva roga nivarini* (the curer of all ailments) while Indian Muslims refer to it as *shajar-e-mubarak* (the blessed tree). The fact that everyone had access to its beneficial properties, even the poorest people, is captured by the Latin name, *Azadirachta indica*, which is derived from the Persian and means 'free tree'.

However, it is possible that Indian citizens will soon be required to pay royalties on products produced from the neem, since a patent has been granted to the US company W.R. Grace, on a compound in the tree (azadirachtin) for the production of a biopesticide. In 1993, over five hundred thousand South Indian farmers rallied to protest against foreign patents on plants such as the neem, and launched a nation-wide resistance movement. Transnational corporations can make large profits on their 'discoveries,' while depriving the communities which have fostered this knowledge for centuries of the beneficial properties of their own flora and fauna.

In West Africa the brazzein berry is renowned for its sweetness. This berry is much sweeter than sugar and, unlike other non-sugar sweeteners, it does not lose its taste when it is heated.

This makes it an ideal candidate for the sugar-free food industry which is worth about $100 billion a year. A US researcher from the University of Wisconsin who saw people and animals eating the berry applied for a US and European patent on the protein isolated from the berry. The drive to create a genetically engineered organism to produce brazzein is under way. This will eliminate the need to grow the berry in West Africa. Naturally, given the market for such a sweetener, there is huge commercial interest in the project.

Most fair-minded people would consider it totally bizarre for the university to claim that brazzein is 'an invention of a UW-Madison researcher'. There are no plans to share any of the benefits of the discovery with the people of West Africa who nurtured this plant for generations.[54] The knowledge, innovation and efforts of these communities are neither acknowledged nor rewarded. Such biopiracy on the part of Northern institutions and corporations should not be legitimised by cleverly worded patenting legislation.

Even when a corporation enters into a deal with a country, such as the well-publicised arrangement between the chemical company Merck & Co and Costa Rica, the benefits which the host nation receives are paltry. Merck has agreed to pay $1 million to the National Biodiversity Institute in Costa Rica in return for being allowed to collect micro-organisms, plants, insects and animals in one of the areas of greatest biodiversity on the planet. Over the long-term the contract could mean billions of dollars profit for Merck. They will only pay a pittance to a Costa Rican research institute. It is worth noting that the indigenous people who live in the forest and whose knowledge of the plant and animals will be crucial in making the agreement work are not included in the deal.

Undoubtedly research into both the food and medical potential of biotechnology will continue in the coming years. The new technology may very well bring benefits to human beings while at the same time promoting a mutually enhancing relationship between our species and the rest of creation. But such an outcome is not at all certain. Therefore, one would like to see the technology accessed not just on narrow scientific or commercial grounds, but on social and ethical grounds also. It is on ethical grounds that the patenting ethos that claims ownership over life is repugnant to many people.

Despite the fact that countries were allowed to exclude patenting living organisms in the Trade-Related Intellectual Property (TRIPs) Agreement of the Uruguay Round of the General Agreement on Tariffs and Trade (GATT) Article 27.3 (b), the whole tenor of the document supports patenting, because it is in the interests of TNCs. Non-government organisations in the North and South should encourage governments to support the following amendment to Article 27.3(b): 'countries must exclude from Intellectual Property Rights plants, animals, micro-organisms and parts thereof, and any process making use thereof, or relating thereto'.

Time magazine (November 30, 1998), discussed the issue of biopiracy and described how an Indian microbiologist who stumbled on a cure which a tribe in the Andaman Islands use for malaria has refused to publish the formula in order to protect the rights of the tribe. An effective cure for malaria would be worth hundreds of millions of dollars for a pharmaceutical corporation. The researcher had hoped that the tribe would benefit from any financial bonanza that might result from the development of a drug. Unfortunately, his superior at a government-run research centre had planned to file a patent for the malaria cure in his own name. As a result the researcher refused to divulge the tribe's secret. The bio-prospecting fever which has gripped many biologists and companies in the wake of patenting legislation will do enormous harm to the well-being of many Third World communities. The only way to effectively defuse this form of genetic imperialism is to repeal much of this recent legislation.

The Precautionary Principle

Given all the above factors, the ethical problems and the risk to human health and the environment the approach to deliberately releasing genetically engineered organisms into the environment ought to be governed by the precautionary principle. This asserts that an action which is risky and could possibly cause widespread and irreversible damage should not be pursued, especially when there is lack of full scientific certainty about the outcome of the action on the organism itself and the wider environment.

Take, for example, the experiment which biotechnologists are now involved in at Newcastle University in Britain. Ruminant animals, like cattle, produce enzymes in their gut which break down cellulose plants into basic sugar components which are then assimilated by the animal. Now scientists are experimenting with introducing cellulose genes directly into nonruminant animals, like pigs and chickens. Their aim is to produce the 'grazing' pig. Whether this would be good for the pigs, given that the rest of their physiology does not suit grazing behaviour, or for the soil structure, is not at all clear. The presumption, based on present knowledge, is that it would not, and therefore the precautionary principle ought to be invoked.

Introducing genetically engineered organism into the environment is very different from introducing other technological inventions. If a chemical and mechanical invention proves dangerous it can be recalled or eliminated. This is not so with genetically engineered organisms. Even if only 1 percent of these organisms wreak havoc on the environment the consequences could be irreversible because the organism will continue to reproduce and thrive. Even before the advent of genetic engineering exotic species that have been introduced into an ecosystem have wiped out indigenous species and interfered with the complex web of relationships which exist between organisms in a complex environment.

Testing

Testing is crucial. Unless you look for something you will not find it. Industry and government spokespersons have been assuring the public that genetically engineered organism are safe. They fail to inform the public that the testing regime is inadequate and often works from quite contradictory positions.

An article in the *New York Times* (October 25, 1998) entitled 'Playing God in the Garden', by Michael Pollan, illustrates how unsatisfactory the present regulatory regime is. Pollan reminds his readers that they may be eating genetically engineered soya, corn or potatoes without knowing it. Even though genetically engineered foods have been on the market for four years in the US the regulatory agency for food, the US Food and Drug Administration (FDA), does not require genetically engineered food be labelled as such.

Today people who eat potatoes in the US cannot be sure that they are not genetically engineered. The author goes on to point out that one of these genetically engineered potatoes Monsanto's New Leaf Superior potato is, itself, registered as a pesticide with US Environmental Protection Agency (EPA). This potato has been genetically engineered to poison and kill the Colorado potato beetle. Every cell of Monsanto's New Leaf Superior contains a gene from the Bacillus Turiengensis bacterium (Bt) which is highly toxic to Colorado potato beetles. This is why this potato is registered as a pesticide.

While the FDA has responsibility for licencing food the US EPA has responsibility for licensing new pesticides. According to Pollan, the EPA pesticide officials believe that the New Leaf Superior potato is reasonably safe for humans. In an experiment EPA scientists fed pure Bt to mice without causing them harm. Because humans have eaten old-style New Leaf potatoes for a long time, and because mice are not visibly harmed by eating pure Bt, the EPA concluded that potatoes containing Bt genes are safe for humans.

The *New York Times* reported that 'some geneticists believe this reasoning is flawed' because, as we have seen earlier in this chapter, inserting foreign genes into plants may cause subtle changes that are difficult to recognize.

When the consumer goes to the supermarket to buy a bag of Monsanto's New Leaf Superior potatoes she/he will find a list of all the nutrients and micronutrients in the potato. He/she will not learn that the potato has been genetically engineered or that it is legally a pesticide. The reason for this anomaly is a bureaucratic bungle: two agencies responsible for human and environmental welfare do not communicate with each other. As we will see, the consumer suffers.

Food labelling is ordinarily the responsibility of the FDA. An FDA official told the *New York Times* that FDA does not regulate Monsanto's potato because FDA does not have the authority to regulate pesticides. According to them that is EPA's job. The farce deepens when one realizes that an EPA-approved pesticides will normally carry an EPA-approved label. For example, a label on a bottle of Bt will warn the user not to inhale the substance or allow it to come in contact with an open wound.

However, in the case of Monsanto's genetically engineered potato, with the Bt gene, the EPA insists that it is the responsibility of the FDA to label the item since the potato is a food and therefore comes under the remit of the FDA. However, an FDA spokesperson told the *New York Times* that it only requires genetically-engineered foods to be labelled if they contain allergens or have been 'materially changed'. In the case of the genetically engineered potato the FDA has determined that Monsanto did not 'materially change' the New Leaf potato by turning it into a pesticide. Therefore no FDA label is required.

Furthermore, the law that empowers the FDA forbids it from including any information about pesticides on food labels. Pesticide labels are EPA's responsibility, says the FDA, which brings us right back to where we started. While two agencies quibble about who has responsibility for what, the consumer is faced with consuming food that is potentially harmful. Neither agency will guarantee the safety of staple foods.

The corporation that produced the potato does not feel that food safety is its responsibility either. A Monsanto official told the *New York Times*: 'Monsanto should not have to vouchsafe for the safety of biotech food,' said Phil Angell, Monsanto's director of corporate communications. 'Our interest is in selling as much of it as possible. Assuring its safety is the FDA's job,' Angell said.

Apart from important decisions falling between various agencies it is also true that US government agencies are very much under-resourced and therefore do not put risk assessment high on their agenda. In 1998 the US Department of Agriculture is still spending only 1 percent of the funds allocated to biotechnology research to fund risk assessment.[55]

In 1997 two researchers, Allison Snow and Pedro Moran Palma, criticized the adequacy of the current field-testing procedures. They argued that since the tests are designed in such a way as to rule out 'gene flow' by insisting on early harvesting or bagging the flowers they are not adequate to access the major risk associated with a large-scale commercial planting of the transgenetic crop. Furthermore, the fact that the experimental area is small and the time scale is limited to one or at the most a few harvests means that there is little possibility to access the negative impact on micro-organisms, insects and plants.[56]

Genetic engineering ought to be treated as the novel process that it is. Regulations ought to be much more demanding and rigorous. Independent verification must be build into the process if it is to regain public trust. Adequate resources need to be put into the regulatory agencies so that the research is thorough.

Problems with national and international regulatory agencies

Is it any wonder that many environmental and consumer groups are very unhappy with national and international regulatory agencies? In the US as we have seen, genetically engineered products do not require a pre-market approval process, public notification, or any labelling whatsoever to inform consumers of their novel and possibly harmful characteristics. The FDA does have the power to regulate food, but in the case of most genetically engineered foods has chosen not to do so. According to the *New York Times* article the FDA maintains a list of foods that need no regulation because they are 'generally recognized as safe' (or 'GRAS'). Since 1992 FDA has allowed companies like Monsanto to decide for themselves whether their new genetically-engineered foods should be added to the GRAS list and thus escape regulation. In other words, FDA regulation of genetically engineered foods is voluntary, not mandatory. This is why The Council For Responsible Genetics claims that a precautionary 'safety proven first' policy has been scrapped in favour of corporate economic interests is very serious indeed.

Industry is essentially placed on an 'honour system,' deciding when and whether to consult with the FDA. Companies conduct safety tests for their own bio-engineered products, notifying the FDA only if they suspect a problem. If they perceive no danger to consumers, companies are not required to state that their product has been genetically manipulated or to reveal the source of implanted genes. They are not required to make the results of their safety tests available to the public.

The FDA will not have a complete set of information regarding genetically engineered foods on the market, so there will be no way to trace who or what is responsible should a problem occur. Not only does the FDA policy forfeit consumers' right to know how their food has been manufactured, it also impedes the public's right to safe and tested food products by allowing the companies who profit from biotechnology to decide if and when a product is hazardous.

More worrying still, consumer and environmental groups also claim that Monsanto, and other corporations, have successfully co-opted national and regulatory agencies to promote their agenda. According to the *St Louis Post*, a current Monsanto vice-president is tipped to become the next Commissioner of the Food and Drugs Administration (FDA) in the United States. The revolving door syndrome whereby high-ranking personnel from the corporate world move into critical positions in the FDA and then back to industry raises questions about the thoroughness and impartiality of the FDA and other regulatory bodies. For example, it transpires that Michael Taylor, the FDA official who wrote the guidelines which prohibits farmers or dairy companies from labelling their milk as free from the Monsanto Bovine Growth Hormone, spent seven years as a Monsanto corporation lawyer.[57] Most citizens would wonder how impartial such a decision might be.

George Monbiot writing in the *Guardian* about the FDA's handling of Monsanto observes that 'the administration has approved some of the company's most controversial products, including the artificial sweetener aspartame and the injectable growth hormone for cattle. Only the New York Attorney General's office has taken the company to task, forcing it to withdraw adverts claiming that RoundUp is biodegradable and environmentally friendly'.[58]

In May 1998 consumer groups, a number of biologists from the University of California and the University of Minnesota, a rabbi, a Protestant minister and a prominent New York restaurant chef filed suit in Washington against FDA policies on genetically engineered foods. They claimed that the FDA had not fully assessed the health risks to consumers and that the regulators had been too eager to let companies market genetically engineered foods with requiring safety tests, or at least, special labels.

Guardian reporters John Vidal and Mark Milner confirmed these criticisms of the regulatory agencies in the final article of a four-day special on biotechnology and food. They found:

- A revolving door between the US government and the biotech industry.
- Heavy lobbying to rewrite world food safety standards in favour of biotechnology.
- New laws protecting the US food industry from criticism.

A further cause for worry is that the corporate reach has moved far beyond the national boundaries to include the decision-making process of multilateral organisations like the World Trade Organisation (WT0). Monsanto has successfully elicited a ruling from the WTO that will make it impossible for the European Union to ban the importation of meat and milk from animals which have been treated with bovine growth hormones even though European consumers, environmentalists and farmers are opposed to such treatment. Consumer confidence is further damaged by claims in *Scientific America* that Monsanto's clinical trials of the drug were incompletely analysed, obscuring the fact that the drug increased the number of infected udder cells in cows by about 20 per cent.

The power of transnational corporations was demonstrated

once again in February 1999 when the US effectively sabotaged a treaty on biosafety in Columbia. The US refused to allow commodities like soya beans and corn to be included in the treaty. If these had been listed they have to be clearly labelled. The US wants to avoid this at all costs because consumers could freely choose not to buy the product.[59]

The publication *GeneWatch* outlines some of the difficulties associated with the current testing regime. These include:

- There is little experience to draw on. All the environmental data so far has been derived from small scale field trials.
- Extrapolating to the wider environment inevitably brings considerable scientific uncertainty given varying climatic and agricultural factors.
- Most trials are designed to evaluate the agronomic characteristics (e.g. yield) rather than the ecological impact.
- Studies are currently conducted on a case-by-case basis neglecting the potential for cumulative impacts (e.g. as ever increasing numbers of herbicide resistant crops are grown).
- With regard to human health, testing has, to date, relied on laboratory studies with laboratory species.[60]

Genetic engineering is very different
from traditional forms of biotechnology

The basis for this lax EPA policy is the inaccurate premise that genetic engineering is only a minor extension of traditional breeding, not significant enough to warrant a unique policy. The bio-engineering industry has opted for the term 'genetic modification; rather than the more accurate term 'genetic engineering'. This has been done to try to convince the public that genetic engineering is a simple logical progression from traditional forms of biotechnology such as making beer, wine, bread and cheese or the practice of selective breeding that human have engaged in since the domestication of plants and animals over eleven thousand years ago. Notice, however, that these type of biotechnology did not involve breeding between completely unrelated species. Traditional breeding never entailed any interference with DNA. No foreign DNA has ever been added or taken away with traditional biotechnology.

Genetic engineering is fundamentally different from these traditional forms of biotechnology, though it is interesting to see that the word 'biotechnology' has been taken over by the biotech industry. Genetic engineering entails the manipulation of an organisms at cellular level to produce an altered organism with whatever desired traits are required. Genetic scientists cut out bits of a living organism's DNA, genes, and splice them into totally unrelated species. As we have seen, animal genes are spliced into plants, bacteria genes are moved across to food crops, and even human genes are used to change animals and plants. The imported genes can destroy or influence the activity of other genes so that a completely new organism is created whose responses in a particular environment are unpredictable.

This cannot be called working with nature in any meaningful sense. It is not natural for one species to cross-breed with a completely unrelated species, or for genetic material to cross over between unrelated species. Genetic engineering manipulates life in ways that could never occur naturally, and places control of evolution itself in the hands of molecular biologists.

That is why it is problematic. Traditional forms of biotechnology leave the natural balance of genes, species and ecosystems intact. Genetic engineering, on the other hand, has the potential to upset this balance irreversibly and to threaten the very diversity of life on our planet.

Genetic engineering circumvents the barrier that exists between different species. It allows for the addition or deletion of proteins in ways not possible through reproduction, creating organisms that are missing essential proteins or harbouring entirely new ones. Genetic engineering brings together genetic material in a way nature never would do. Nevertheless the FDA chose to treat transferred genes as natural food products as long as they come from an approved food source, thereby failing to consider the unpredictable effects which the old gene may have in its new system.

At the international level, the joint *Safety Report on Genetically-engineered Foods* issued in 1996 by the Food and Agriculture Organisation (FAO) and the World Health Organisation (WHO) decided that the WHO's *Codex Alimentarius* Commission will decide on the safety of genetically engineered foods. Risk assessment will be based on the 'principle of substantial equivalence' developed by the Organisation for Economic Co-operation and Development (OECD). This means that 'if a new food or food component is found to be substantially equivalent to an existing food or food component, it can be treated in the same manner with respect to safety'. This principle has been severely criticised by many scientists as totally inadequate. The tests for substantial equivalence are so undiscriminating that, according to Dr Mae-Wan Ho, 'unintended changes, such as toxins and allergens, could easily escape detection'.[61]

Labelling

The FDA must require industry to notify them when any genetically engineered food goes on the market. In the event of problems, this would provide a 'trail' for scientists, medical personnel and regulators to follow in order to determine the origins of an unsafe product.

Opinion polls in Europe and elsewhere indicate the public want clear and informative labelling of genetically engineered foods. A basic step in honouring this consumer preference is to segregate genetically engineered foods from natural foods at source. Many of the corporations that produce genetically engineered foods are opposed to segregation and labelling. They claim that it would be too expensive since it would involve using different containers, trucks and warehouses. They protest that their products are safe and have latched on to the concept of 'substantial equivalence'.

The focus here is not on how the food was produced, whether from natural or genetically engineered seeds, but on the chemical nature of the food. Should a chemical analysis of the food or food ingredient find that the product is substantially the same as the naturally produced one, no label should be required on safety grounds. In fact no label should be used at all as this might be interpreted as discriminating against genetically produced foods. According to the agribusiness corporations, genetically engineered foods are no different from naturally produced food.

However consumer groups and scientists are unhappy with the notion of substantial equivalence. They cite the process that led to the BSE epidemic and argue that sheep products fed as protein supplement to cattle would probably have passed the substantial equivalence test, yet the presence of prion proteins led to a public health disaster. As has been highlighted earlier, toxicity and allergenicity might not turn up in laboratory experiments for substantial equivalence.

It is clear from a *Guardian* poll in June 1998 that people want to know whether the food they eat is derived from genetically engineered products. In response to the question whether 'foods that have been genetically modified should be clearly labelled', 96 per cent answered Yes. In 1997 a similar opinion poll in the US commissioned by Novartis found that 97 per cent wanted all biotech food labelled. The Consultation Paper by the

Department of the Environment recognises that 'from a consumer point of view, the information currently being provided is inadequate to facilitate clear choices on whether or not to purchase products containing GMOs or products using genetic modification techniques'.[62]

The only way to achieve this satisfactorily is to segregate genetically engineered food from non-genetically engineered at source. Otherwise there will be problems, even if mandatory labelling for genetically engineered food is introduced. Without segregation, for example, tomato paste from genetically engineered tomatoes would have to be labelled, but a processed food like lasagne that contained genetically engineered tomatoes would need no label. Mandatory labelling of all genetically engineered food products should be required by law and not left to the retail outlets.

Segregation and clear labelling are the minimum necessary to ensure product safety and protect a consumer's right to choose whether or not to purchase these products. Consumer groups all over Europe and the United States are calling for such a system. Once again, in the matter of labelling, the public are poorly served by the regulatory agencies. In response to the research that a soybean that contained a Brazil nut caused an allergic response in the trial group an editorial in the prestigious medical magazine *The New England Journal of Medicine* chided the FDA in the US for its unwillingness to demand verifiable and across-the-board labelling. The editors stated that it appeared that the FDA 'favour industry over consumer protection'.[63]

The decision by some retail outlets to label with the words 'may contain genetically modified products' means very little. If there is no segregation almost all processed food might contain some genetically modified substances. In practice this would prevent the consumer from exercising her or his choice of choosing foods that are not genetically engineered.

The wealth and political power of the biotech industry

It should not come as a surprise that many biotech companies have opposed segregation and mandatory labelling. The companies know that, in a post-BSE world, the public want to know where and how their food is produced. Many consumers are willing to pay extra to ensure that the products they buy are produced naturally. This would be bad news for the biotech industry. Given the huge investment which companies like Monsanto have made they need to gain significant market share quickly or else cash-flow problems will send their shares tumbling on the stock market.

Monsanto went on a buying spree in 1996 and 1997 and invested $2 billion buying up dozens of biotech companies, including Calgene of Flavr Savr, in order to gain control of their research patents. Many believe that their ultimate aim is to produce and patent genetically engineered varieties of all staple food crops. These new crops are created to out-produce existing varieties and might be expected to dominate this particular market globally within a short period of time. In the process farmers will become reliant on the patented seeds of the biotechnology industry. As shown above, the industry has now developed seeds that will not germinate when replanted.[64] Monsanto now owns this patent.

After buying out or taking control of many small, innovative biotech companies, including Delta Pine, Monsanto turned its attention to large seed distribution corporations. In 1997 Monsanto bought Holden's Foundations Seeds for $1.2 billion. A year later in June 1998 it paid a record £843 million for Cargill International. This huge agribusiness has sales and distributions networks in fifty-one countries on four continents. This acquisition will give Monsanto huge control of global seed markets. It will also become the conduit for distributing their GE seeds. Farmers will have very little option but to buy these GE products. Within a few short years the transition to GE crops will be accomplished. If the strategy works the profits for Monsanto will be astronomical.

It is no wonder that the *Guardian* correspondent, George Monbiot, fears that 'with astonishing rapidity a tiny handful of companies is coming to govern the development, production, processing and marketing of our most fundamental commodity: food. The power and strategic control they are amassing will make the oil industry look like a corner shop' (*Guardian*, 17 September 1997). It is frightening to think that within a few years the world's food supply could be dominated by eleven or fewer giant Northern controlled agribusiness corporations. In 1998, 81 per cent of the global agrochemical market was controlled by ten companies. The stakes in the present scramble for market share in genetically engineered products are enormous. The global market for one year is estimated to be worth $400 billion.[65]

Monsanto have engaged in a high-wire financial operation that could end in financial disaster. They have chosen a risky option in putting most of their financial eggs into the biotechnology basket. If consumers shy away from genetically engineered food this could prove very costly for biotech companies, especially Monsanto.

Writing in the business section of *The Independent on Sunday* (12 May 1996) Paul Rodgers noted that biotech companies have been the darling of the stock market in recent times. But he struck a note of caution. He quoted a market analyst Peter Doyle as being 'surprised by the values attributed to companies on the basis of prospects rather than products'.

This explains the headlong rush to get genetically engineered products on to the supermarket shelves as soon as possible. Yet this may prove more difficult than we have been led to expect. For every genetically engineered product that has a commercial value there are twenty or more that simply fail. By mid-1998 the biotech companies were experiencing some organisational difficulties and were are beginning to slip again on the stock markets.

This is why companies like Monsanto are desperate for quick results. They need to turn their investment into a steady flow of profits or their bankers might begin to ask questions and their share-price might slump. Because of the potential pitfalls the future of biotechnology should not be dictated by the commercial interest of companies like Monsanto, but by concern for the welfare of people and the planet.

The power that large corporations like Monsanto can wield over elected governments is a very disturbing development in recent decades. Such companies with financial resources greater than many countries are poised to make huge profits if the biotechnology enterprise prospers and replaces other more traditional technologies in agriculture and medicine. Governments that are elected to promote the well-being of their citizens should be wary about the risks involved and should regulate and monitor the industry much more thoroughly to protect the health of the people and the environment.

A number of recent developments are very worrying indeed. In January 1999, *The Sunday Tribune* reported that during the visit of the Taoiseach, Bertie Ahern, to the US in March 1998, leading figures in the US administration, including Sandy Berger, the director of the US National Security Council, used the Taoiseach's visit to try to influence Ireland's vote about the upcoming decision about planting crops engineered for insect resistance. Politicians 'including Senator Christopher Bond collared Ireland's Prime Minister on the subject' according to a report in *The St Louis Post Dispatch*. Some commentators described as worrying and frustrating 'the access Monsanto had to the Taoiseach during the visit'.[66] It would be very difficult for Mr Ahern to brush aside overtures from US administration personnel or politicians given the pivotal role the US had played in the Northern Ireland peace process. Could it be that such hard-nosed lobbying by US and Irish biotech industry probably accounts for the fact that Fianna Fáil quietly dropped the hostility that they had to genetic engineering while in opposition?

Similar apparent conflict of interests can be seen in the Labour government's approach to biotechnology in Britain. On February 12 1999 a report in *The Guardian* claimed that research carried out by Dr Arpad Pusztai at the Rowlett Research Institute in Scotland, which showed that rats fed on genetically engineered potatoes had suffered significant damage to their vital organs, had been suppressed. Dr Pusztai believed that the cauliflower mosaic promoter used in the experiment might be the cause of the harm. The story broke after twenty-two prominent scientists had backed the professor's research and queried why he had been forced to take early retirement. The incident raised many disturbing questions. The *Daily Mail* headline on February 14,1999 – 'Gene Lab Took Food Giant's Gift' – claimed that Monsanto had given a £140,000 gift to the institute. Could such a gift influence the way decisions were made about research findings at the Institute?

More worrying still was the potential conflict of interest of the science minister Lord Sainsbury. As head of the supermarket chain, Lord Sainsbury had strenuously promoted GE foods. In fact he owns a number of valuable patents which are used in creating GE foods. The Blair government insisted that Lord Sainsbury had done nothing wrong and that he had taken no part 'in any government decisions on discussions relating to GM food policy'.[67] A letter-writer to *The Guardian*, February 17,

1999, put his finger on the real problem. The author, Dr Anthony Dowd, pointed out that 'the recent ruling by the law lords on the Pinochet case was disallowed as one of their number had links with a human rights group. The link between several members of a government committee considering GM food (Lord Sainsbury included) and the biotechnology industry don't seem to have led to a conflict of interests. This surely is a case not only of injustice being done, but being seen to be done'.

It also appeared that the Minister for Agriculture had given £13 million to the biotech industry to help improve its public image and inspire confidence among consumers. In the summer of 1998 Mr Cunningham and his deputy, Mr Jeff Rooker had held meetings with Monsanto. The meeting was arranged by Bell Pottinger who is a public relations consultant for Monsanto. In October Cathy McGlynn, formerly a special adviser to Mr Cunningham, joined the Monsanto team.[68] Here, once again, we see the revolving door system at work. People have a right to ask: Whose interests are being served?

In the US biotech companies like Monsanto wield enormous power. The company has made huge donations to both the Republican and Democratic parties and pays lobbyists to represent its interests both at state and national level. It has made financial contributions to Congressmen who sit on food safety and regulatory committees. Within the US political system this is, unfortunately, quite legal. Mickey Cantor who was the chief US negotiator during the Uruguay Round of the GATT negotiations and the chairman of Bill Clinton's 1992 presidential election campaign now sits on the board of Monsanto. Monsanto has also made huge contributions to President Clinton's Welfare-to-Work programme.

According to Betty Martini who belongs to consumer group Mission Possible which monitors Monsanto's activities in the US, 'The Food and Drug Administration, which regulates the

US food industry, is so closely linked to the biotech industry that it could be described as their Washington branch office'.[69] John Vidal also states that there is a 'constant exchange of staff between the government, the company and the regulatory bodies'.[70] An analysis of Monsanto's operations in the US and globally in the *St Louis Post-Dispatch* in December 1999 stated that 'where Monsanto seeks to sow, the US government clears the ground'.

Monsanto can engage in much more aggressive lobbying when they perceive that their interest are threatened. In 1993 a memo was prepared for a Monsanto executive, Tony Coehlo, in preparation for a crucial meeting with the US Agriculture Secretary, Mike Espy. The memo was written by Dr Virginia Weldon and approved by Monsanto's chief executive, Robert Shapiro. The purpose of the memo was to threaten Secretary Espy that 'if the Clinton administration does not stand up to persons like Senator Feingold' Monsanto will likely pull out of agricultural biotechnology. Senator Feingold's offence in the eyes of Monsanto was that he was attempting to secure a moratorium on the use of their Bovine Growth Hormone until further test had taken place. Daniel Jeffreys wrote in the *Daily Mail* (18 February 1999) that the memo then continues chillingly: 'The administration must let socio-economic factors dictate approval of a new product'. Jeffreys comments that 'in other words, not health considerations, not safety issues, but profits'.

Given this open approach to politicians and regulators it is understandable that until recently there has been very little opposition to GE foods in the US. The biotech companies paved the way for public acceptance of the technology by investing heavily in 'educational' material in schools during the late 1980s and early 1990s.

Opposition to GE crops is more persistent in Europe

Opposition to GE foods has been much more vigorous in Europe. It seems that Monsanto misjudged the reaction of European consumer concerns over genetically engineered products. A study in Germany in 1998 found that only 15 per cent favoured GE food while 81 per cent were opposed to it. In April 1998, Philip Angell, Monsanto's US director of corporate communications stated: 'We made a mistake which we regret. We should have listened more carefully'. Environment organisations see this talk of listening and of openness to dialogue with the opposition as merely another ploy to speed up acceptance of genetically engineered products by consumers.[71]

In October 1998, the *New Scientist* carried a report that other biotech companies were very critical of the tactics used by Monsanto in Europe. These companies feel that Monsanto is 'largely to blame for a consumer backlash that could cripple the prospects for genetically engineered food in Europe ... A high-profile advertising campaign from Monsanto, designed to reassure European consumers, has, if anything, hardened negative public attitudes to agricultural biotechnology. "We are as fed up as some others with the Yankee-Doodle language that comes to our consumers," says Greef of Novartis'. The Advertising Standards Authority (ASA) in Britain condemned Monsanto's advertising campaign for making claims about GE foods that were 'confusing, misleading, unproven and wrong'. Claims that GE crops were grown in environmentally sustainable way were also dismissed, and the suggestion that Monsanto would sacrifice sales of its herbicide RoundUp to reduce pesticide use when it had no intention of doing so, was 'confusing'.[72]

At a debate in University College, Dublin, on 'Ethics and Genetic Engineering' one of the speakers in favour of the industry claimed that horror stories in the media were responsible for turning people against the technology. My own experience of the media is much closer to Jeremy Rifkins's. He contends that the US media have, by and large, accepted the warm 'glowing' arguments in favour of the biotech industry uncritically. The media have trumpeted many of the break-throughs on the 'genetic frontier, with little effort to examine the more complex risks, pitfalls, and dangers that accompany the biotech revolution- issues that cry out for public airing as we turn the corner into the century of biology'.[73]

In 1999 the Government is being lobbied by the biotech industry with claims that the future belongs to biotechnology and that the industry has the potential to produce thousands of jobs, surpassing the job-creating achievement of the computer industry. Such claims should be sifted assiduously. Until re-cently Ireland was known for fresh, clean food, produced in an environmental friendly way. We should be resolute in our determination to protect the healthy image of food production here in Ireland. The image has taken a bit of a battering with the outbreaks of BSE and the use of growth hormones in cattle in recent years. It would be folly at this point to allow genetically engineered food to be grown and further erode our green image. If something went wrong this would spell disaster for the whole Irish food industry.

Who benefits from genetically engineered food?

One might ask who benefits from GE food? Is it the consumer? Are they demanding this kind of food technology? The answer would seem to be a resounding No. A survey on *Consumer Attitudes to Genetic Engineering and Food Safety*, commissioned by the environmental organisation Genetic Concern was car-ried out in Ireland by Lansdowne Market Research in January 1999. The survey found that very few people felt that they were well informed about genetic engineering. 78 per cent said that they knew little or nothing about the technology. Most of those who felt they were well informed – 89 per cent – were concerned about the implications of genetic engineering for food safety. Only 8 per cent were unconcerned. Generally speaking, women, especially married women, were more concerned than men. This is hardly surprising since women do the bulk of the weekly shopping. When asked whether they were concerned about genetic engineering, a clear majority of those interviewed said they were.

Another voice expressing concern is Mr John McKenna, a food writer with the *Irish Times*, who told the Irish Association of Health Stores that the consumers do not want GMOs in their food. 'There is no demand from any quarter other than the producers of GMO food' (*The Irish Times*, 20 October 1997).

Such foods first began to appear a few years ago. Now the consumer is faced with a flood of genetically modified organisms appearing on the supermarket shelves. The range covers foods that contain genetically engineered rape seed oil, soybeans, maize, sugar beet, squash, potatoes and cucumber. More than half the processed foods on the supermarket shelves contain soya in one form or another. An opinion poll carried out by *The Guardian* in Britain in June 1998 found that 50 per cent of those asked were not happy with the introduction of genetically modified foods, while only 14 per cent were happy.

Despite their resistance consumers are left with little choice. Many companies that sell soybean, for example, have refused to segregate genetically engineered soybeans from ordinary soybeans. As a result the consumer is being forced to eat food that is genetically modified, often without knowing that the product contains genetically engineered soya.

One supermarket chain, Iceland, with 770 stores in Britain and six in Ireland, has decided to ban all foods containing genetically engineered organisms. The founder and chief executive, Malcolm Walker, has accused biotechnology companies of 'conning' Irish and British consumers and claimed that genetically engineered food is being introduced 'by stealth'. Health food shops in Britain are also determined to rid the shelves of produce that might contain GE ingredients. The policy extend to sauce mixes and vegetarian burger mixes.[74]

Between 1995 and 1998 the proportion of supermarket products that contained GE ingredients jumped from zero to 60 percent, mainly because most pre-prepared foods contain GE soya beans and GE corn. both of which are widely used in almost all pre-pared foods. The change occurred because of the dramatic swing among US soya growers from traditional soya to GE soya. It seemed only a matter of time before the GE juggernaut swept everything away in its path. Neither seed producers like Monsanto or the giant supermarkets reckoned with consumer hostility to GE food products, especially in Europe.

The backlash against GE foods was so strong, especially in Britain where they were called 'Frankenstein Foods' by that tabloid press that in the Spring of 1999 almost all the leading supermarkets including Asda, Marks and Spencer, Sainsbury and Tesco pledged to eliminate GE ingredients from their own-brand food products. In April food producers like Unilever, Cadbury and Nestle followed suit in the face of consumer pressure.[75]

In the mid-1999 the hostility to GE foods spread to Japan and South America. In August two leading brewers In Japan, Saporro and Kirin, announced that they would stop using genetically engineered corn by within two years. In Mexico the leading producer of corn-flour for tortillas decided it would no longer buy GE corn.[76] The impact of this on GE farmers in the US has been devastating. Instead of GE crops being less troublesome and delivering greater profits, as touted by the corporations like Monsanto and government advisers, they are causing financial ruin for many. The price of GE soya has plummeted which non-GE soya is now fetching premium prices as supermarkets scour the world looking for non-GE soya beans.

Irish supermarket chain Superquinn that markets itself as specialists in fresh food, published a pamphlet on genetically modified food early in 1999. It accepts that the biotech-industry argument that there is a direct continuity between food modification using 'either natural or biotechnological means'. It proclaims that the 'benefits from genetically modification are manifold and include disease resistant crops; crops that require less herbicides and pesticides in their production; longer lasting fruits and vegetables, and foods with higher vitamin, mineral and protein contents and lower fat contents'. The document admits there are concerns but it does not list them in the way it lists the so-called benefits. Superquinn promises that it will label foods that are 'genetically modified or produced from genetically modified soya and genetically modified maize'. However, they will not label 'oils or other soya and maize derivatives ... as they do not contain certain modified protein'. They claim that 'the oils are identical to the oils from the non-modified seeds and they do not contain genetic material'. Here we are back to the equivalence debate. The producers will not be forced to segregate the soya at source. However, in the summer of 1999, Superquinn followed its British competitors and agreed to ban GE ingredients from its own brand food.

One boost to the campaign to ban GE foods has come from leading cookery writers like Darina Allen. She is one of a hundred leading cooks and food writers who is demanding GE-free food. In Ms Allen's view 'genetic engineering is not a precise science. There is no turning back, no second chance. We must be sure we are right and, if that means waiting 25 years, so be it'.[77]

If the pressure to grow and eat genetically engineered food

is not coming from the consumer, where is it coming from? Both John McKenna and Dr Eddie Walsh of UCD agree that the push is coming from biotech companies like Monsanto that have invested huge amounts of money and stand to make the most out of the technology.[78]

It is worth pointing out that according to the United States Department of Agriculture 98 per cent of the modifications to date have been undertaken for commercial reasons. This includes extending the shelf-life of a product as in the case of the Flavor Savr tomato or making crops resistant to a patented herbicide. Virtually none of the modifications are designed to improve nutrition.

Call for a moratorium on the deliberate release of genetically engineered organisms

Given the difficulties associated with genetically engineered organisms there is good reason to insist on a five -year moratorium on the deliberate release of genetically engineered organisms until the risks are much clearly understood and there is a thorough public discussion of all the issues involved. The moratorium must include a ban on the commercial growing of GE crops, the importation of GE food and ingredients and their use in human and animal feeds.

At a seminar on biotechnology during the Biosafety Meeting in Montreal in May 1997 a delegate from West Africa asked: 'How old is the oldest transgenetic line?' None of the scientists present could answer his question. Dr Mae-Wan Ho claims that there are 'no data documenting the stability of any trangentic line in gene expression, or in structure and location of the insert in the genome'.[79] She goes on to stipulate that 'such data must include the level of gene expression as well as the genetic map and DNA base sequence of the insert and its site of insertion in the host genome for each successive generation. No such data have every been provided by the industry, nor requested by the regulatory authorities'. Until such information is available at least over a five-year period it makes all kind of sense to insist on a moratorium.

The Union of Concerned Scientists in Washington in their 1993 report on genetic engineering, entitled 'Perils amidst the Promise', also promote the idea of a moratorium. They concluded that no company should be permitted to commercialise a transgenetic crop in the United States until a strong government programme is in place that assures risk assessment and control of all transgenetic crops. They also call for adequate protection for the centres of crop diversity in the US and elsewhere in the world.

Austria has imposed a two-year moratorium on field trials of genetically engineered organisms. One million, two hundred thousand people, representing 20 per cent of the population, signed a petition supporting a ban on genetically engineered foods, as well as a moratorium on the deliberate release of genetically engineered organisms. Switzerland held a referendum on genetic engineering on June 7, 1998. After a bitterly fought campaign the voters decided to reject a proposal to ban the patenting and production of genetically altered plants and animals. Unlike other countries, at least the people of Switzerland had an opportunity to decided the matter for themselves.

In the wake of the controversy surrounding Professor Pusztai's findings on GE potatoes fed to rats forty environmental and religious organisations in Britain called for a five-year ban on GE food. This call for caution seems eminently reasonable given the fact that the issues are so grave and the dangers of getting it wrong are so serious.

The story of the African Killer Bee ought to foster caution. A noted Brazilian geneticist, Warwick Kerr, was experimenting with the bees when it accidentally escaped into the wild. This happened in the late 1950s. The bee has now spread throughout South and Central America and is moving north in the United States with devastating results for the environment and people.

Such dramatic failures by scientists themselves should breed caution. Recombinant DNA techniques has delivered enormous power into the hands of a small group of people in the biotechnology corporations where profits often tend to take precedence over everything else. For this reason the public should make sure that a lot more is known about the safety of genetically engineered organisms before any group in society is allowed to begin to tinker in an extensive and impactful way with the building blocks of life. There should be a full-scale public debate on both the benefits and risks involved in genetic engineering based on comprehensive scientific knowledge and a full airing of the economic, social and ethical implications of biotechnology.

Ireland should follow the Norwegian model in deciding whether we adopt genetically engineered organisms or not. In 1996 Norway adopted a consultation model on biotechnology which was developed by the Danish Board of Science. In the process groups of ordinary people assessed the various aspects of biotechnology including the ethical, economic, political, social and legal perspective, in addition to the narrower technological considerations before deciding whether Norway should opt for biotechnology. The panel concluded that 'there was no need for genetically modified food in Norway today, because the selection, availability and quality of ordinary food is satisfactory. Too many uncertain factors attach to genetic engineering'.

We would do well to follow this example until much more is known about genetically engineered organisms. Unfortunately the consultation process set up in Ireland by the Minister for the Environment was totally unsatisfactory from the perspective on the participating NGOs. Minister Dempsey announced at the beginning of the process that he had ruled out a moratorium since it was contrary to EU law even though Luxembourg and Austria have already declared a moratorium. The NGOs also felt that the debate with the biotech industry was superficial and lacked any depth. It was very poorly structured and amounted to little more than an exchange of sound-bites. For this reason the majority of NGOs withdrew from the process. It came as no surprise to the NGO community that the Consultation, published in October 1999 [80] came down on the side of the biotech industry in Ireland. The Report misrepresents the biocentric ethical argument when it states that it seeks 'the well-being of the comprehensive community as opposed to the well-being of the human community'. (p. 22) This is not at all what is involved as is clear from pages 130 to 137 of this chapter.

It is ironic that just as the Irish government is about to embark on pro-industry biotech policies despite the overwhelming need for caution, the British government is seeking peace talks with environmentalists and consumer groups. This time they are seeking a genuine dialogue. [81] The Irish government should pursue a similar course so that there is a thorough, comprehensive debate on genetic engineering before releasing this technology into the environment.

CHAPTER SEVEN

The Eucharist – Renewing the Covenant

Over the past decade Christians, in common with people of other faiths and none, have become more and more concerned about the extensive and, often, irreversible destruction of the environment in their own locality and on a global scale. They have been encouraged by the leadership of the World Council of Churches and by Pope John Paul II to become more aware of environmental issues and to support concrete programmes and initiatives to protect and restore the integrity of creation.

In his World Day of Peace message for 1990, entitled *Peace with God the Creator, Peace with All Creation*, the Pope reminds Catholics that 'their responsibility within creation and their duty towards nature and the Creator are an essential part of their faith' (n. 14). While recognizing the complexity of environmental questions the Pope highlights the moral and religious aspect of the crisis.

The Catholic Church, however, has been slower to recognize the energizing power which good, imaginative liturgy might have in transforming the way Christians relate both to other human beings and to the rest of creation. While it is generally recognized that there is an urgent need to move away from the exploitative, mechanistic view of nature to a more compassionate and sustainable way of relating to the natural world the contribution of liturgy to promoting this process is hardly adverted to at all. While everyone accepts that good ritual is first and foremost an act of worship of God, nevertheless sensitive liturgies can also help the process of reconciliation with nature, especially for people living in an urban environment who no longer have an intimate, dependant relationship with nature.

Focusing on the cosmic or ecological aspect of liturgy is hardly new. Since the dawn of human history men and women have sought to express how the deepest mysteries of their lives and the values of their society are bound up with the rhythms of the earth and the cosmos. They have done this through the medium of myths and rituals. These ceremonies often embody both the highest artistic expression of a people and their deepest insight into the meaning of life, and thus have a powerful impact on the culture.

Within the Catholic tradition, the Eucharist has, since apostolic times, been such a celebration. While it is abundantly clear that the texts and rituals used in celebrations of the Eucharist have evolved over time in response to particular historical or cultural pressures, all commentators are agreed that the Eucharist has been central to Christian life since apostolic times. Given this fact and the particular ecological challenges today, it is strange that, while the new *Catechism of the Catholic Church*[1] is clear that the 'Eucharist commits us to the poor', it is silent on the relationship between the Eucharist and the imperilled creation. At the same time, theologian and liturgical scholar David Power is conscious that the ecological question was overlooked by those involved in reform of the liturgy. He writes: 'other factors that have been inadequately considered in liturgical reform are [the] impending ecological travail'.[2]

In this chapter I will focus on two themes – covenant renewal and thanksgiving to God for all God's gifts, including the gift of creation. By developing these themes, and the ethical positions that they support within contemporary Eucharistic celebrations, Christian communities can develop 'creative forms of worship that are both genuinely new cultural creations and in continuity with an ancient tradition'.[3] As David Power points out, in the Christian generation immediately after the time of the apostles, Justin Martyr, justifying the celebration of Eucharist on Sunday, 'associates the Eucharist itself with the creation of the world and with the resurrection of Christ'.[4]

Renewing the Covenant

The narrative of the institution of the Eucharist in Mark's Gospel – 'This is my blood, the blood of the covenant, which is poured out for the many' (Mk 14:24) – indicates clearly that the Eucharist is understood as the renewal of the covenant sacrifice. The worshipping community recalls Christ's passion, death and resurrection, and experiences the transforming power of his presence.

Covenant (*berith*) was a social and juridical mechanism whereby groups or individuals in the ancient Near-East established and maintained relationships. The agreement between an overlord and his vassal, often called the suzerainty covenant, provided the contours within which Yahweh's relationship with Israel was framed and developed.

That covenant-form included a number of important elements. The senior party or overlord displayed his beneficence by the very fact that he was willing to enter into a relationship with someone inferior to him. The preamble normally listed the acts of kindness, protection and support that the sovereign has already displayed towards the underling. Next, the vassal signified his willingness to be of service to the king and to obey him. Finally, the covenant was sealed with a ritual that often involved a blood sacrifice or a meal.

All of these elements are present in the covenant that Yahweh entered into with Israel at Sinai. The Sinai covenant recognizes the fact that it is Yahweh who reaches out to invite a group of wandering people fleeing from oppression in Egypt to become a community of worshippers of God, dedicated to his service and willing to obey his laws. The text in Exodus 19 goes on to summarise Yahweh's great deeds in rescuing his people from oppression and slavery and promising to lead them into a new and fertile land: 'You yourselves have seen what I did with the Egyptians, how I carried you on eagle's wings and brought you to myself' (Ex 19:3-4). A positive response is then requested of the people – to 'obey my voice and keep my covenant'. Indeed the Sinai covenant is made conditional on this. Finally, the text of chapter 24 mingles two tradition for sealing the covenant. One involves sprinkling the blood on the altar that represented Yahweh and on stone pillars representing the twelve tribes of Israel; and the other involves a meal in the presence of God.

In the Hebrew Scriptures the Sinai covenant acts like a fulcrum. It links the earlier covenants, like the ones with Noah and Abraham in Genesis, with later covenants, for example, the one with David and his descendants in 2 Samuel 7. It is also the touchstone to which the prophets will constantly return to strengthen their call for renewal and repentance particularly when the poor and underprivileged are exploited and oppressed (Am 5: 21-27). The prophet Isaiah is equally blunt and dismissive of ritual that does not promote sharing and community building.

The New Testament sees the fulfilment of the Covenant in the life, death and resurrection of Jesus. The word 'covenant' is used in the four accounts of the Last Supper (Mk 14:17-25, Mt 26:20-29, Lk 22:14- 23, and 1 Cor 11:23-33). It is clear from the words, 'This cup is the new covenant in my blood' (Lk 22:20), that Jesus sees his impending death as the fulfilment of a new and irrevocable covenant between human beings and Yahweh that was foretold by the prophet Jeremiah (Jer 31:31-34). His life, death and resurrection are the new mighty works of God that secure, not political freedom and a promised land, but the inauguration of the Kingdom of God.

The sacrificial nature of Jesus's act if clear from the fact that his blood is 'poured out' (Lk 22:20). The text recalls the fact that the blood of sacrificial animals was used to seal the Covenant at Sinai and also alludes to the vocation of the Servant of Yahweh who bore our sufferings and carried our sorrows and whose own life was 'poured out' in service of the many (Is 53:4.12). The new Covenant which is sealed by the once-for-all sacrifice of Christ is renewed for the Christian community in Eucharistic Celebrations carried out in fulfilment of the mandate of Jesus to 'do this as a memorial of me' (1 Cor 11:25, Lk 22;19). By eating his body and drinking his blood the members of the Christian community unite themselves in an intimate body with the offering of Christ, making it present in their time and place: 'until the Lord comes, therefore, every time you eat this bread and drink this cup, you are proclaiming his death' (1 Cor 11:26).

While the 'mighty deeds' of Yahweh – which are celebrated in most of the covenants in the Hebrew Scriptures and even in the New Testament – focus on God's saving deeds in the human realm, God's magnificent work of creation provides the background for these covenants. On occasions, especially in the covenant with Noah (Gen 9:8-18) creation is explicitly included. The covenant with Noah is established not merely with Noah and his sons and daughters but with every living creature. Yahweh points to the rainbow as a sign of 'the covenant I have established, between myself and every living thing that is found on the earth' (Gen 9:17). The Jesuit biblical scholar Robert Murray in his book *The Cosmic Covenant* believes that celebrations of a cosmic covenant designed to repel hostile forces and promote harmony and righteousness across the social, religious and cosmic domain were also important in Israel.[5]

The integrity of this cosmic covenant is very much under threat today. The danger comes not from demiurges or evil spirits but from human activity on earth. Environmentalists today point out that modern economic patterns of production, distribution, consumption, trade and development are taxing and even breaching the regenerative capacity of the biosphere and its ability to absorb human created pollution. In very crucial areas it is shredding the integrity of creation. The Harvard biologist, Edward O. Wilson estimates that at the moment we are losing 27,000 species each year. That means seventy-four each day or three every hour.[6] This sterilization of the earth involves a diminishment of life for all future generations of human beings and other creatures. It means extinction for hundreds of thousands or even millions of species within a relatively short period of time. It is, in fact, the most destructive impact on the web of life since the end of the Mesozoic period of the earth's history sixty-two million years ago.

As we have seen, in the Sinai Covenant the people of Israel were challenged to live by the light of God's word and God's law, the Torah. Similarly the new Covenant in Jesus's blood calls Christians to follow a way of life – his example of love. One important dimension of this in our contemporary celebration of the Eucharist is the call to be much more sensitive to the destruction we are wreaking on creation. Renewing the covenant today in our Sunday Eucharist invites us to formulate a new Decalogue which takes cognizance the ecological crisis.

Many contemporary efforts have been made to develop an ecologically sensitive morality. These involves moving beyond the horizons of inter-human behaviour to examining the moral component of human interaction with the rest of the natural world. As we have seen in the chapter on Ethics and Genetic Engineering, the American environmentalist Aldo Leopold in his well-known essay 'Land Ethic' set out to expand the boundaries of the ethical community to include human behaviour towards 'soil, water, plants and animals, or collectively; the land'. For Leopold, human acts that promote diversity and stability in the biotic community are considered moral and good while actions that undermine a biotic community are deemed immoral.

The Dutch writer, Louke wan Wensveen Siker, has attempted to develop and ecologically sensitive code by examining the traditional virtues and vices through the prism of the present ecological crisis.[7] According to her, traditionally, the sin of pride focused on individual behaviour. It dealt with the conceit and arrogance of a person who attempted to set himself or herself above every one else, including God. From an ecological perspective, pride or *hubris* has a social and species dimension as well as an individual one. Such a spirit of *hubris* often leads humans to think of themselves as the only species with real value on the planet. We mistakenly think that no other species deserves respect or consideration. Furthermore we often declare that every other creatures is created primarily to serve human needs and can be exploited to meet either our needs or our whims. The spirit behind the development of much of modern science and, especially, technology is also permeated with this sense of hubris. We feel that once we humans have discovered how to do something, we have every right to experiment with nature even we are not fully aware what the consequences might be for other humans and the rest of creation.

Elsewhere in this book I argue that genetic engineering is a good example of this *hubris*. Humans feel that they have right to re-design other species to serve humans more efficiently even when the procedures involve gross exploitation of other creatures.

Pride on this scale is pillaging, degrading and destroying the world. It needs to be counteracted by acquiring, individually and collectively, a profound sense of humility. The derivation of this word 'humility', from the Latin *humus*, meaning soil, should provide a salutatory corrective. It should remind us that, like every other creature on the planet, we are creatures of the soil and responsible to God for our actions.

A more humble attitude in the face of creation will remind us that science and technology are valuable when they seek to understand nature and work in harmony with its stupendous technologies. They are harmful to both humans and the rest of creation when, in order to deliver some short-term benefits to individuals or groups, they destroy the Earth.

Professor Siker has an interesting comment on sloth. This vice hardly seems capable of an ecological interpretation. She links it with the vices of *tristitia* (melancholy, or pessimism) and *acedia* (apathy or lack of care for others). Pessimism and even despair often seem justified in the light of rampant ecological devastation. Yet they are totally useless if anything positive is to be done to preserve any part of creation; and they also fly in the face of Yahweh, the God of surprises and revolutions, whose commitment to life is most obvious in Jesus's triumph over sin and death. Such a resistant faith tempered in suffering, failure, death and resurrection can energize people to commit themselves to major lifestyle changes in the way they use energy and the other resources of creation.

Finally, the work of Marshall Massey is worth mentioning. He has captured the flavour of this new ethical perspective in his ecologically sensitive Decalogue which he published in the Quaker magazine *The Friends' Bulletin* in 1985. The religious language echoes the Book of Exodus but the content is grounded in a deep knowledge of ecology and of the current environmental crisis. A few examples will illustrate what is involved. The prologue states:

> I the Lord am the God that made you; and as I made you, so have I made all living things, and a fit place for each thing, and a world for all living things to share in interdependence.

Some of the ecologically sensitive prescriptions include:

> You shall not act in any way which makes the world less able to sustain life;
>> not by destroying the soil,
>> not by destroying the living seas,

not by laying waste the e wild places,

not by releasing poisons,

not by causing great changes in the climate.

You share not act in any way that injures the buffers I have set about this world to protect its life;

the ozone layer of the atmosphere,

the carbon dioxide sink of the sea,

the chemical balance of the waters,

the interface between water and sky,

the vegetative cover of hill-sides and plain,

the multitude of species in a region,

the balance of species each with each,

and the adaptability of species as contained in their genes.

If the Sunday Eucharist on a number of occasions each year could be seen to highlight the renewal of the cosmic covenant theme and evoke the kinds of moral behaviour contained in such a decalogue then the Eucharist celebration could have a powerful impact in promoting work for justice and the integrity of creation among Christians.

Eucharist

We can also pursue an ecological approach to the Mass by focusing on the meaning of Eucharist. The word 'eucharist' comes from the Greek word *eucharistia* which means thanksgiving. The origins of the prayer of thanksgiving at Mass lie in the prayer of blessing and thanks (*berakah*) over food which a presider at a Jewish meal would proclaim, especially meals which had explicit religious overtones like the Passover. It is worth noting that as well as *eucharistia* another Greek word was needed, *eulogia*, meaning blessing, to capture the full blessing-thanksgiving nuances of the Hebrew word *berakah*. This blessing-thanks attitude for the gift of food was naturally deepened when the prayer of *berakah* encompassed all the wonders that

Yahweh had accomplished for the people, especially his loving kindness in rescuing them from Egypt and embracing them in a covenant bond.[8]

Modern scholarship views the Last Supper not as a Passover meal but as one of those formal religious meals called *chaburah* which a circle of friends might share once a week.[9] Still, the prayers of blessings used at the *chaburah* are influenced by the Passover themes. And at the particular *chaburah* in which Jesus 'longed to keep this Passover' (Lk 22:15) before he would suffer, Passover overtones were intensified by that fact that the synoptic Gospels place the institution of the Eucharist within the celebration of the Passover meal (Mk 14:12-16). They are also present in John's account of the last supper (Jn 13:1- 18.26) even through his chronology of events is different (Jn 18:28; 19:14.31).

The Passover meal emerged from a fusion between the a festival of a pastoral people who sacrificed of a young kid from the flocks to evoke God's blessing on the flock and the pastoral community (Ex 12:3-6), and a similar festival by a farming people where the offerings included unleavened loaves and the first-fruits of the harvest (Lev 23: 5-14). It comes as no surprise that a communion meal is central to both festivals. For subsistence farmers, who regularly experience the swings between hungry periods when food is scarce and times of plenty after harvests, food and drink take on a special sacred value. This was certainly true in the demitic world.

Whatever about its origins, the Passover meal in which a lamb was consumed with unleavened bread and bitter herbs was celebrated as a remembrance of Yahweh's love in liberating the people of Israel from oppression and exploitation in Egypt. Yahweh's mighty power struck at the heart of Egyptian arrogance by inflicting plagues on the Egyptians culminating in the death of their first-born. Yahweh's power was swift and decisive. The people were told to eat with 'a girdle round your waist, sandals on your feet and a staff in your hand. You are to eat it hastily; it is the Passover in honour of Yahweh' (Ex 12:10-11). When the youngest child asked the father 'what does this ritual mean? you will tell them, 'it is a sacrifice of the Passover in honour of Yahweh who passed over the houses of the sons of Israel in Egypt, and struck Egypt but spared our houses' (Ex 12:26-27).

The father of the house proclaimed the *haggadah* or the story that encompassed all that Yahweh had done for Israel down through the centuries. In this prayer of blessing and thanks (*berakah*), God's action was not seen as something that happened in the dim and distant past to one generation of Israelites and was merely commemorated by their descendants. No, in the Passover meal every generation of Israelites experienced liberation and came out from Egypt.

The *anamnesis* or remembrance at the heart of the Christian Eucharist, celebrated within the context of a meal, recalls God's greatest act of love, which unfolds in the life, death and resurrection of Jesus. 'God loved the world so much that he gave his only Son, so that everyone who believes in him many not be lost but may have eternal life (Jn 3:16).

Gregory Dix in *The Shape of the Liturgy* points out that 'the Jewish berakah, from which all eucharistic prayers are ultimately derived, did give thanks to God for His natural bounty in the first paragraph, as well as for the blessings of the Covenant in its second'.[10] Thanking God for the gifts of creation is present in eucharistic prayers from the very beginning. In the eucharistic text found in the *Apostolic Tradition* of Hippolytus that dates from around 215 A.D., it appears in second paragraph immediately after thanking the Father for sending Jesus Christ as Saviour and Redeemer.[11]

Creation also figures in contemporary eucharistic prayers. Eucharistic Prayer II in the Missal of Paul VI echoes the words of Hippolytus when it proclaims that '[Jesus] is the word through whom you made the universe'. Eucharistic Prayer IV thanks the Father for all the blessings of creation: 'Source of life and goodness, you have created all things to fill your creatures with every blessing and lead all [people] to the joyful vision of your glory'. Eucharistic Prayer III, on the other hand, instead of thanking God for creation, focuses on the fact that all creation is called to praise God: 'Father, you are holy indeed, and all creation rightly gives you praise'. The Roman Canon itself alludes to creation when it states that 'from the many gifts you have given us we offer to you, God of glory and majesty, this holy and perfect sacrifice: the bread of life and the cup of eternal salvation'.

The most elaborate development of the creation theme is found in Preface 33 (for Sundays of the Year, V). It links the creation of the world with the creation of human beings and highlights the vocation of human beings to be stewards of creation:

All things are of your making,
all times and all seasons obey your laws,
but you chose to create man in your own image,
setting him over the whole world in all its wonder.
You made man the steward of creation,
to praise you day by day for the marvels of your wisdom and
    power,
through Jesus Christ our Lord.

Given the crisis that faces creation today, the fact that creation plays a minimal role in the eucharistic prayers is unfortunate, and change is needed. But the problem goes beyond the infrequent reference to creation in the liturgy and includes the particular perspective on creation that is found in the liturgy.

For a variety of historical and theological reasons the liturgical texts on creation are based almost exclusively on the Bible, especially the early chapters of the book of Genesis, or to a lesser extent the Fathers of the Church. These texts can and, often do, promote a caring attitude toward all creation. Nevertheless, the hierarchical structure of the Genesis 1:1-2:4a, with its static, unchanging features and its human-centredness contrasts with the dynamic, evolutionary and inter-dependant vision of creation which emerges from the insights of modern biology, botany and genetics.

Modern science describes how the universe emerged from the mysterious fireball. It tells how the elements were forged in the galactic cauldrons of the first generations of stars and they collapsed in supernova explosions. It tells how these new elements seeded the our solar that gave rise to our sun and the planets, especially, Earth. It tells how, over hundreds of millions of years our earth was formed in its physical dimensions. Finally, it tells how life arrived on earth first as a tentative flicker and later in great profusion and diversity, culminating in the emergence of a reflectively self-conscious creature, called *homo sapiens*.

The details of this fascinating journey, gleaned from the data of the natural sciences has, in recent times, been woven into an emergent, dynamic story by people like Thomas Berry and Brian Swimme.[12] The general contours of this story are available to students in all modern schools whereever science is taught. Various aspects of the story also feature regularly on the media. Television is particularly well suited to explaining and illustrating the story as we see in the great variety of nature and natural history programmes that have appeared in recent years. Programmes like David Attenborough's *Life on Earth* which narrates the story of evolution and *The Living Planet* that explores how life, in its different forms, has adapted to a variety of climates and topographies, are fascinating and have drawn huge audiences. Many people, especially young people, are captivated by the story of the dinosaurs.

In May 1995, Radio Telefís Éireann (RTÉ) presented a series of programmes on Ireland called *Written in Stone*. This documentary, through a combination of striking shots and the use of models, presented an extraordinary insight into how the landmass which is now the island of Ireland was formed. It tells how it rocks were shaped, convulsed, eroded, submerged, thrust up and reshaped scores of times. It is an engrossing story that expands the imagination as the viewer contemplates the scale and duration of the processes involved in begetting his/her local environment.

On the following Sunday if the person who has moved by viewing such a programme attends the liturgy he/she will either hear no reference to creation. If creation is mentioned it will be a static viewpoint that bears little resemblance to the perspective which has been presented so graphically on the television natural history programme. The disjunction between the new understanding of creation in school and in the media and the static story of creation in the liturgy is not healthy. Faced with this seeming contradiction there is a danger that worshippers will simply dismiss the biblical revelation as antediluvian and irrelevant without giving any thought to important insights it contains. There is also a danger of an increasing sense of alienation between everyday life and worship.

An attempt has been made to weave these two traditions together into a eucharistic prayer. In May 1984 the first eucharistic prayer composed in English was published by the International Commission on English in the Liturgy (ICEL). The text, especially the Preface, set out to capture in poetic language the beauty, inherent dynamism and inter-relatedness of all creation:

Blessed are you, strong and faithful God.
All your works, the height and the depth,
echo the silent music of your praise.
In the beginning your World summoned light;
night withdrew and creation dawned.
As ages passed unseen,
waters gathered on the face of the Earth
and life appeared.
When the times had at last grown full
and the earth had ripened in abundance,
you created in your image humankind,
the crown of all creation.
You gave us breath and speech,
that all the living might find a voice to sing your praise.
So now, with all the powers of heaven and earth,
we chant the ageless hymn to your glory ...

This text combines the insights of a modern evolutionary perspective with the biblical notion that humans are stewards of creation. It is, of course, merely a first step in re-invigorating liturgy with creation themes. Future texts might seize on what Thomas Berry calls the cosmological 'moments of graces'. These refer to crucial moments in the universe story – the explosion of the supernova stars which created many of the elements that combine to make our world, or that moment when life first dawned, or when flowering plants burst forth. A eucharistic prayer might recognise these sacred moments as 'mighty works of God' to be celebrated alongside God's compassion in rescuing the Israelites from slavery in Egypt.

Unfortunately at present such creative developments are not possible. Even the mildly evolutionary overtones in the ICEL text proved unacceptable to some bishops. Admittedly ten out of eleven of the bishops' conferences represented in ICEL had no problem with the text and approved it. Even so the US Bishops' Conference voted it down on the grounds that 'it seemed too poetic and too imbued with evolutionary images of creation'.[13] As a result of the US Bishops' action Rome refused to sanction the text for public use. Sadly this text is now confined to Eucharistic Celebrations which take place at creation-theology workshops.

We can only hope that this short-sighted decision by the US hierarchy will soon be reversed. The decision was made before they published their statement on the environment, *Renewing the Earth: An Invitation to Reflection and Action on the Environment in the light of Catholic Social Teaching*, in November 1991. In 1994 the US Catholic Conference prepared a resource package for parishes which dealt with the theological, pastoral and liturgical aspects of the environmental awareness and action. As the Church in the United States travels down this trail of growing environmental awareness and action it will have to explore how the new story written in the rocks and the flora and fauna relates to and complements the story of creation which is contained in the Bible. The eco-theologian, Jay B. McDaniel in his book *With Roots and Wings* strives successfully to combine insights from the new scientific story told by Thomas Berry and the biblical account.[14] Once this journey is undertaken with an open mind I feel the ICEL Eucharistic Prayer will be approved.

I would like to see ICEL Eucharistic Prayer become a prototype for other, even more, localized eucharistic prayers. Such eucharistic prayers ought to dwell on, not just the general outlines of the emergence of the earth as God's gift, but they should praise and thank God for the shape, beauty and fruitfulness of the locality in which the Eucharist is being celebrated. A truly inculturated eucharistic prayer would dwell on God's action in shaping of a particular ecosystem be that a river, a lake, an estuary coastal zone, wild boglands, picturesque mountains, rich pasture, farmlands or urban environment.

Such eucharistic prayers would draw on local natural history, culture and a localized theology of creation. Liturgy rising from this milieu would, through the use of poetic language, images, gestures, music and dance, reconnect a worshipping people with their immediate landscape. Like the songlines of Australian aborigines, liturgies would become powerful signposts on the road to re-establishing an intimate relationship between human beings living in a particular place and the rest of creation.

If a local ecosystem is under stress from human, agricultural or industrial pollution the heightened awareness of the preciousness of that local gift of God, incorporated into a eucharistic prayer, would act as a powerful stimulus to the community to protect and preserve their God-given heritage.

An illustration of what I have in mind comes from my own locality. I was born in North Tipperary less then three miles from Lough Derg. This is the largest lake on the Shannon river and the second largest lake in Ireland. During the past twenty-five years the quality of water in the lake has deteriorated through a combination of agricultural pollution and municipal and industrial waste. The input of nutrients has led to algal blooms during warmer weather. Water, that a generation ago was clear and fit to drink, takes on the texture of light green pea-soup during the warm summer period. For generations people enjoyed swimming in the lake. During recent summers the green, slimy, foul smelling sludge in many of the bays of the lake have deterred swimmers from taking the plunge.

The growth of algae depletes the oxygen in the water. This leads to a deterioration in the quality and diversity of aquatic life of the lake. In previous times the lake was famous for its brown trout. This too has changed. Catches have dropped dramatically in recent years. In 1993 a citizens' group called

Save Our Lough Derg (SOLD) to put pressure on politicians at the national and local level to take the deterioration of the lake seriously. Numerous reports indicate that the root causes of the problem need to be addressed in a comprehensive and effective way. The various components of the solution at a technical, political and financial level have been identified. These will involve schemes to reduce the entry of phosphorous and nitrogen into the lake or tributaries through improved farming and better waste treatment plants.

Though many of those involved in attempting to rehabilitate the lake are Catholics, little consideration has been given to the spiritual dimension of this life-system. Its waters have nourished plant and animal life, including human life, in the catchment area, for thousands of years. The lake itself, with its wide expanse, its different moods, its profusion of animals, birds, fish and insects and its invitation to silence and solitude, has played an important, though largely unrecognized, role in the emotional and spiritual life of the inhabitants in the area. A local eucharistic prayer, developed by a creative dialogue between local pastoral agents and local artistic talent would thank God for the waters of the lake and its enchanting surroundings. Such worship would energize Catholics in their efforts to restore the lake before extensive and irreversible damage takes place.

It is obvious that creation themes offer opportunities for Christian communities in different parts of the world to praise and thank God for their own environment and for developing appropriate ethical norms for relating to the earth. In this way Christians nourished by a life-enhancing liturgy will be inspired to shed an exploitative attitude towards nature and become effective stewards on behalf of all the community of nature and the landscape.

The particular form of these prayers and liturgies will depend on the people's own experience of nature, the riches of

their own historical and cultural tradition and current knowledge about nature and environmental problems. In Ireland, for
example, early Christian Celtic spirituality which was so sensitive to the presence of God in all of nature, can be utilized to help
overcome the alienation which many modern people, brought
up in an industrial age, feel towards nature. This sympathetic
understanding towards nature came from a careful knowledge
of it. Kuno Meyer who did so much pioneering work on Celtic
literature, wrote that 'to seek out and watch and love Nature, in
its tiniest phenomena as in its grandest, was given to no people
so early and so fully as to the Celts'.

In many countries in Asia, Africa and North and South
America the experiences, practices and insights of tribal or
indigenous peoples into the dynamics of creation can be shared
with the majority population and enrich their liturgical celebrations. For most tribal people nature is not inert or mechanistic.
They do not view it primarily from a utilitarian perspective as
a quarry from which to extract the resources which humans
need for their well-being and enjoyment and as a dump in
which to consign their waste. For most tribals the Earth is alive
with the spirits of many different beings and the spirits of the
ancestors. Nature has its own value and dignity, apart from its
value to human beings, and that should be respected and
revered. I saw for myself the intimate relationship between
tribal peoples and their environment during the years I lived as
a missionary among the T'boli people of South Cotabato in the
Philippines.

The creation stories in Genesis stress the chasm that divides
humans and the rest of creation. In Genesis 1:26 humans are
seen to be unique. They and they alone are made 'in God's
image and likeness' and they are designated 'to be masters of
the fish of the sea, the birds of heaven, the cattle, all the wild
beasts and all the reptiles that crawl upon the earth'. The second

account of creation, from the Yahwist tradition, also stresses the gulf between humans and the animals. The creation of man precedes that of the animals (Gen 2:7). In an effort to find a helpmate for the man Yahweh created the animals and invited the man to name each one of them (Gen 2:19-20a). The power to name in Semitic culture is not merely a right to designate what name an individual or animal should have. Names describe the inner being and proper role of a person, animal or entity and indicate their place in society or the cosmos. As it turned out 'no helpmate suitable for man was found for him' among the animals (Gen 2:20b).

Given the enormous diversity which is found among tribal peoples in different parts of the world any generalization about them is almost invariably incorrect. Nevertheless tribal creation stories are often more holistic, and feature a kinship between all the beings of the earth which echoes the truth that we now know from the story of the universe that everything in the universe is connected to everything else.

A few examples of holistic understanding of our world will suffice. In a creation story from Banks Islands, north of New Hebrides in Melanesia, Qat, the local cultural hero, and his eleven brothers are born from a stone. The holistic metaphor is continued when Qat formed people out of trees and inspires them with his sacred drumming.[15] The Cheyenne of the Great Lakes in North America view the earth as a grandmother. Trees and grass spring from grandmother's hair and flowers are her bright ornaments.[16] At the end of the second millennium when the diversity of life is very much under threat, these stories can enrich liturgies in different parts of the world. They will help to enkindle among the worshippers a spirit of kinship with all creatures, small and great, that is so important for our time.

Finally, the gifts we use in the Eucharist, bread and wine, symbolize not only the gifts of creation, wheat and grape juice, but the human dimension of care and creativity involved in fashioning these elements into food and drink. In a very real way the gifts offered at the Eucharist become a symbol of that mutually enhancing relationship between humans and the rest of creation that modern humanity so needs to develop if we are to attain a truly just and sustainable world. The Eucharist is a symbol of that social world where we are supported and sustained by the labours of others. In the bread that is broken and the cup that is shared is an invitation to build a just world. David Power, reflecting on the meaning of bread and wine, especially for those who are in need, writes that in attending Eucharist gatherings we are 'faced by [the] ritual with issues of human need and human justice'.[17] We should also be faced with issues of the 'earth's suffering'. What better place to express this than in the Eucharist which is a true memorial of Christ's suffering and death. In such a context the Eucharist will challenge Christians to create patterns of human living especially in the economic and social sphere, that are sensitive to other creatures and ecologically sustainable. This may well be ritually expressed in incorporating, once again, the role of lament within the Eucharistic celebration. As corn-crakes, yellowhammers, corn buntings and clean, potable water disappear from the Irish landscape there is much to lament.

Finally, the Eucharist is also an anticipation of the Spirit renewing all creation when God's rule will be established. But that yearning for the future coming of the Lord who is encountered in the Eucharist must not be seen an excuse for inaction or passivity. Rather should challenges those who share table fellowship to work for fellowship with all creation.

Notes

INTRODUCTION

1. Franz König, 'The Pull of God in a Godless Age' *The Tablet* 18 September 1999, p. 1250.

2. Kevin O'Sullivan, 'Problems of the Environment Are Intensifying – EPA', *Irish Times*, 15 July 1999, p. 14.

3. Bishop Bill Murphy, *Going to the Father's House: a Jubilee People*, Pastoral Letter to the Diocese of Kerry 1999.

4. For text see 'And God Saw It Was Good', *Catholic Theology and the Environment*, ed. Drew Christiansen, S.J., and Walter Grazer, (Washington, D.C., USCC 1996.

CHAPTER 2
Cancelling Unpayable Thrid World Debt

1. Charlotte Denny, 'Mitch's Victims Call for Relief,' *The Guardian*, 9 December 1998, p. 15.

2. Susan George, *The Debt Boomerang*, 1992, London, Pluto Press, pp. xv-xvi/

3. Larry Elliott, 'Why the Poor Are Picking up the Tab,' *The Guardian*, 11 May 1998, p. 6.

4. ibid., p. 24.

5. John Vidal, 'Slaves in Our Land' – A Tale of Two Sams,' *The Guardian*, 15 May 1998, p. 1.

6. Quoted in Naom Chomsky, 'The People always Pay', *The Guardian*, 15 May 1998, p. 7.

7. Davic Pallister, 'For 5pc of £200 You Get a Head of State,' *The Guardian*, 15 May 1998, p. 6.

8. Robert J. Samuelson, 'The Crash of 98?', *Newsweek*, 12 October 1998, p. 39.

9. Quoted in *State of the Nation A Comprehensive Statement on the Current Situation in Zambia*, by the Catholic Commission for Justice and Peace, PO Box 31965 Lusaka, p. 11.

10. The statistics used in this discussion on Zambia are taken from *Zambia: Debt vd Development*, 1997, The Debt and Development Coalition Ireland, All Hallows, Grace Park Road, Dublin 9.

11. Editorial, 'The Debt Crisis R.I.P,' *The Economist*, 12 September 1992, p. 23.

12. Duncan Campbell, 'Bolivia: Battered on All Sides by the Habit of a Lifetime', *The Guardian*, 15 May 1998, p. 5.

13. Archbishop Antonio Jose Gonzalez Zumarraga, 'Foreign Debt Problems in Latin America,' *L'Osservatore Romano*, 10 December 1997.

14. Bruce Rich, *Mortgaging the Earth: The World Bank, Environmental Impoverishment and the Crisis of Development*, 1994, Boston, Beacon Press, p. 26.

15. Susan George, *The Debt Boomerang*, 1992, London, Pluto Press, pp. 8-9.

16. Tim Radford, *The Diversity of Life*, 1992, Harmondsworth, Penguin, p. 256.

17. Tim Radford, 'Wearing the World Away,' *The Guardian*, 9 March 9, 1995, p. 4.

18. The Paris Club is the name given to the representatives of creditor governments who meet, in secret, to discuss rescheduling bilateral debts, under the chairmanship of the French finance minister.

19. Charlotte Denny, *The Guardian*, 9 December 1998, p. 15.

20. A CAFOD briefing paper 'A Human Development Approach to Debt Relief for the World's Poor' Henry Horthover, Karen Joyner and David Woodward, June 1998, p. 2.

21. Jo Marie Griesgraber, 'Jubilee 2000 a Bold Call for Forgiveness of Debt', *Center Focus*, Setpemebr 1998, p. 2.

22. Larry Elliott, 'Fury at G8's Debt "Failure",' *The Guardian*, 2 April 1998.

23. Alex Brummer, 'Clinton Wipes Debt Slate', *The Guardian*, 30 September 1999, p. 27.

24. *Newsletter of the Debt and Development Coalition Ireland*, June 1998, p. 1.

25. Jeffrey, Sachs, 'the IMF and Asian Flu' , *American Prospect*, March-April 1988: quoted in Larry Elliot and Alex Brunner, 'One Size Does Not Fit All', *The Guardian*, 3 July 1998.

26. Quoted in Martin Khor, 'Confronting Chaos', *Multinational Monitor*, October 1998, p. 10.

27. Mark Atkinson, 'Survival Training for the Labour Market' *The Guardian*, 1 February 1999, p. 19.

CHAPTER 3
Global Warming

1. Tim Radford, 'It's Getting Hotter – and There's No Escape', *The Guardian*, 12 August 1998, p. 2.

2. 'Global Warming Blamed for Erosion as Beachy Head Starts to Crumble into the Sea', *The Irish Times*, 13 January 1999.

3. Windstorm, Munich Re Special Publication, 1990 in *The Climate Time Bomb*, Greenpeace International.

4. *Sign of Peril, Test of Faith*, A Study Paper from the World Council of Churches, 1994, Geneva, p. 11.

5. ibid., p. 11.

6. Paul Hawkins, *The Ecology of Commerce*, HarperCollins, 1993. New York,p. 183.

7. Frank McDonald, 'Irish Levels Will Rise by 28% "Unless Policy Changes"', *The Irish Times*, 1 December 1997, p. 11

8. Pul Brown, 'Millions May Die in Global Warming', *The Guardian*, 22 October 1998, p. 12.

9. Frank McDonald, 'Are We Serious?', *The Irish Times*, 20 September 1997, p. 7.

10. *Accelerated Climate Change: Sign of Peril, Test of Faith*. A study paper from the World Council of Churches. 150, Route de Ferney, P.O. box 2100, 1211 Geneva 2, Switzerland.

Chapoter 4 God Called the Waters Seas

1. Bradford Matsen, 'If the Present Rate of Extinction Continues, 70 percent of All Corals Will Be Dead in 20 to 40 Years,' *Mother Jones*, May 1998, p. 62.

2. Don Hinrichsen, 'The Ocean Planet,' *People and the Planet*, 1998, pp. 6-7.

3. Originally published in *Science*, February 1998 and quoted in Peter Montague, 'Oceans without Fish,' *Third World Resurgence*, April 1998, p. 5.

4, Kevin O'Sullivan, 'Action on Sea Pollution Sought to Ensure Survival of Marine Species,' *The Irish Times*, 21 July 1988, p. 3.

5. Kevin O'Sullivan, 'Sellafield Ordered to Curb Discharges as States Agree Sea Pollution Pact,' *The Irish Times*, 24 July 1998, p. 24.

6 Bruce McKay, 'Cleaning up the Seas,' People and the Planet 1998: 16.

7. Norman Habel, *The Land Is Mine*, 1995, Minneapolis, Fortress Press, p. 190.

8. John Eaton, *The Circle of Creation*, 1995, London, SCM Press, pp. 1-116.

CHAPTER 5
Living Downwind from Hiroshima and Chernobyl

1. John Vidal, 'The Last Blast', *The Guardian*, 16 December 1993, pp. 12-13.

2. *The Defense Monitor*, vol. XXII, no. 1, 1994, Centre for Defense Information, Washington D.C.

3. Frank Pitman, 'Navajos-UNC Settle Tailings Spill Lawsuit', *Nuclear Fuels*, 22 April 1985.

4. Audrey Magee, 'Chernobyl Radiation Persists in Ireland', *The Irish Times*, 26 April 1996.

5. Kathy Sheridan, 'One in Four or Five Is Expected to Develop Thyroid Cancer, instead of One in a Million', *The Irish Times*, 15 April 1996, p. 6.

6. Scott Sullivan, 'Nukes for Sale' *Time*, 29 August 1994.

7. 'Nuclear Shut-Down Is a Financial Time Bomb', *The Ecologist*, January-February 1988, pp. 9-14.

8. Paul Brown, 'BNFL Fined £20,000 for Disregarding Safety', *The Guardian*, 15 April 1997, p. 6.

9. John Vidal, 'The Last Blast', *The Guardian*, 16 December 1993, p. 13.

10. 'Worried about What's Floating in the Irish Sea? Things Are about to Get a Whole Lot Worse', *The Evening Herald*, 3 February 1994, pp. 30-31.

11. 'Dundalk Residents Given the Right to Sue BNFL on Sellafied', *The Irish Times*, 31 March 1995, p. 8.

12. Don Hinrichsen, 'Russian Roulette', *Aisling*, August 1993, pp 68-71.

13. International Atomic Energy Agency, General Conference, twenty-sixth regular session (20-24 September 1982), record of 240 plenary meeting held in Neue Hofburg, Vienna.

14. 'Wise Atomic Energy Plan Is Needed', *L'Osservatore Romano*, 30 September 1991.

15. Michael Andersen and Paul Brown, 'Nuclear Replacement for Chernobyl' *The Guardian*, 17 February 1999, p. 13.

CHAPTER 6
Genetic Engineering

1. Robert, Steyer, 'Monsanto Refuses to Pay $1.94 Million to Farmers,' *St Louis Post-Dispatch*, 20 June 1998, p. 3.

2. Aristotle, *Politics*, Harmondsworth, Penguin, 1985 edition.

3. Keith Thomas, *Man and the Natural World*, 1983, New York, Pantheon Books, p. 35.

4. Clive Ponting, *A Green History of the World*, 1991, London, Sinclair-Stevenson, p. 142.

5. Stephen Mason, A History of the Sciences , 1962, New York, Collier Books, p. 27.

6. Jeremy Rifkin, *Time Wars*, 1987, New York, Henry Holt, p. 176, quoted in Andrew Kinbrell, *The Human Body* , 1993, Harper San Francicso, p. 237.

7. David Suzuki, 'Can Science "Manage" Nature?' *The Ecologist*, January/February 1998.

8. Roisín Ingle, 'Bellamy Happy To be a Bogman', *The Irish Times*, 4 April 1998, p. 10.

9. Eugene Linden, 'How the World Waited too Long to Rescue the Shield

That Protects Earth from the Sun's Dangerous UV Rays,' *Time*, 10 May 1993, pp. 56-58.

10. Hans Küng, *A Global Ethic for Global Politics and Economics*, 1997, London, SCM Press, pp. 91-113.

11. John Polkinghorne, 'The Unity of Truth in Science and Theology', in Science and the Theology of Creation, Church and Society Documents, No 4, August 1988, page 31.

12. The Report of a Working Party of the Catholic Bishops' Join Committee on Bioethical Issues, *Genetic Intervention in Human Subjects*, 1996, London, Linacre Centre, p. 10.

13. T.F. Cross and P.T. Galvin, *The Nature and Current Status of Transgenetic Salmon* (Dublin: Marine Institute of Ireland, 1996) p. 6.

14. Jeremy Rifkins, *The Bioethic Century*, 1998, London, Victor Gollanz, p. 97. Rifkins cites Langley, Gill, 'A Critical View of the use of Genetically Engineered Animals in the Laboratory', in Wheale and McNally (eds.) *Animal Genetic Engineering*, London, Pluto Press, pp. 194-188.

15. Dieter T. Hessel, "Now that Animals can be Genetically Engineered',' Ecotheology (New York: Orbis Publications, 1995) p. 285.

16. Aldo Leopold, *A Sand Country Almanac*, 1994, New York, Ballantine Books, p. 239.

17. ibid., p. 262.

18. Bill Davis and George Sessions, *Deep Ecology: Living as if Nature Mattered*, 1985, Salt Lake City, Gibbs, Smith, p. 64.

19. Thomas Berry, *Ethics and Ecology*, unpublished paper 1994.

20. Quoted by Dieter T. Hessel in 'Now that Animals Can be Genetically Engineered: Biotechnology in theological-Ethical Perspective', *Ecotheology*, New York, Orbis, p. 204. Original quotation in James A. Nash, *Loving Nature: Ecological Integrity and Christian Responsibility*, 1991, Nashville, Abingdon, pp. 61-62.

21. Editorial, 'The Need to regulate and control genetic engineering,' Third World Resurgence No 53/54: 17.

22. Jeremy Rifkins, *The Biotech Century*, 1998, London, Victor Gollanz, p. xi.

23. Editorial, 'Some critical environmental issues after Rio,' Third World Resurgence No. 81/82: 19.

24. Mae-Wan Ho *et al.*, 'The Biotechnology Bubble', *The Ecologist*, vol. 28, no. 3, May/June 1998.

25. Mae-Wan Ho, 'The Unholy Alliance,' *The Ecologist* vol. 27, no 4, July/August 1997, p. 156.

26. Alan Simpson, 'Soul Ownership', *Resurgence*, May/June 1998, p. 14.

27. Mae-Wan Ho, Harmut Meyer and Joe Cummins, 'The Biotechnology Bubble,' *The Ecologist*, May/June 1998, p. 149.

28. James Meikie, 'BSE Warning That Was Ignored', *The Guardian*, 1 April 1998, p. 1.

29. Phyllida Brown, 'Pig Transplants 'Should Be Banned",' *New Scientist*, March 1997, p. 6.

30. Michael Day, 'Tainted Transplants: Pig Organs May Never Be a Safe Replacement for Desperately Scarce Human Livers', *New Scientist*, 18 October 1997, p. 4.

31. Quoted in Rifkins, p. 87. Original reference; Rissler and Mellon, *The Ecological Risks of Engineering Crops*, 1996, Cambridge, MA, MIT Press, pp. 34-40.

32. G.R. Squire, D. Burn, and J.W. Crawford, 'A Model for the Impact of

Herbicide Tolerance on the Performance of Oilseed Rape as a Volunteer Weed', *Annals of Applied Biology*, 1997, pp. 315,338, quoted in *GeneWatch*, May 1998.

33. US National Biotechnology Impacts Assessment Programme Newsletter, March 1991. 'The Case of the Competitive Rhizobia'. Taken from the Greenpeace website.

34. Mae-Wan Ho and B. Tappeser, 'Transgenic Transgression of Species', prepared for a workshop on transboundary movements of living modified organisms resulting from modern biotechnology, Aarhus, Denmark, 19-20 July 1996.

35. Joseph Mendelson, 'RoundUp: The World's Biggest-Selling Herbicide,' *The Ecologist*, September/October 1998, p. 272.

36. Richarda Steinbrecher, 'What Is Wrong with Nature?', *Resurgence*, May/June 1998, p. 18.

37. Greenpeace International Glyphosate Fact Sheet, November 1996.

38. Quoted in *GeneWatch*, May 1998, p. 2.

39. Factsheet from Genetic Concern entitled *RoundUp!RoundUp*, April 1998.

40. Pat Roy Moody, 'Private Parts: Privatisation and the Life Industry'. *Development Dialogue*, 1998, p. 147.

41. Nicholas Schoon, 'Genetic-crop Threat to Wildlife Survival,' *The Independent*, 25 March 1998.

42. Jeremy Rifkins, *The Biotech Century*, p. 73.

43. Gauri Lankesh and Pallavi Ghosh, 'Indian Farmers Burn Genetically-engineered Crops' *Third World Resurgence*, December 1998/January 1999, pp 2-4.

44. Sean Poulter, '£17,000 Fine That Will Take 90 Seconds to Pay', *Daily Mail*, 18 February 1999, p. 9.

45. H.W. Kendall, R. Beachy, T. Eisner, F. Could, R. Herdt, P.H. Vaven, J. S. Schell, and M.S. Swaminathan, 1997, *Bioengineering of Crops: Report of the World Bank Panel on Transgenic Crops*, International Bank for Reconstruction and Development/World Bank, Washington D.C.

46. Robert Shapiro, 'Growth Through Global Sustainability', *Harvard Business Review*, pp. 79-88.

47. Christopher Leaver, 'Novel Ways to feed the world' The Guardian, February 17,1999, page 8.

48. *Ecologist*, September/October 1997, pp. 211-212.

49. Pat Roy Mooney, 'First Parts: Putting the Particulars Together,' *Development Dialogue*, April 1998, p. 70.

50. Quoted in John Vidal, 'Mr. Terminator Ploughs in ', *The Guardian*, 14 April 1998.

51. Jean-Pierre Berlan and Richard C Lewontin, 'It's Business as Usual', *The Guardian*, 22 February 22, 1999, p. 14.

52. Andrew Kimbrell, *The Human Body Shop*, 1993, San Francisco; Harper, p. 190.

53. Vandana Shiva, "The Enclosure of the Commons", Third World Resurgence, August 1979 , page 6.

54. 'Patenting, Piracy and Perverted Promises: Patenting Life; the Last Assault on the Commons', *Grain Girona* 25, pral, E-08010 Barcelona, Spain, pp. 5-6.

55. Rifkins, p. 77.

56. Rifkins, p. 78

57. Daniel Jeffreys, 'The Record That Shames the Biotech Bully Boys', *The Daily Mail*, 18 February 1999, p. 8.

58. George Monbiot, 'Watch These Beans,' *The Guardian*, 7 October 1997.

59. Jeremy Lennard, 'Washington Kills Global Pact to Govern GM Trade', *The Guardian*, 23 February 1999, p. 14.

60. GeneWatch, MAY 1998. PAGES 4-5.

61. Mae-Wan Ho, Hartmut Meyer and Joe Cummins, 'The Biotechnology Buble,' *The Ecologist*, May/June 1998, p. 146.

62. *Genetically Modified Organisms and the Environment: A Consultation Paper*, Department of the Environment, Dublin, August 1998, p. ix.

63. Jeremy Rifkins, *The Biotech Century*, (London, Victor Gollancz, 1998), p. 105.

64. Wayne Brittenden, '"Terminator" Seeds Threaten a Barren Future for Farmers,' *The Independent*, 22 March 1998, p. 3.

65. John Vidal and Mark Milner, 'Big Firms Rush for Profits and Power despite Warnings,' *The Guardian*, 15 December 1997.

66. Claire Grady, 'Ahern Lobbied on Modified Crops,' *The Sunday Tribune*, 3 January, 1999, p. 3.

67. Ewen MacAskill and Tim Radford, 'Blair Insists Sainsbury Stays; Government Tries to Allay Public's Fears on GM Food', *The Guardian*, 17 February 1999, p. 1.

68. George Monbiot, 'Stop the Crops', *The Guardian*, 14 February 1999, p. 21.

69. Julian Borger, 'Why Americans Are Happy', *The Guardian*, 20 February 1999, p. 4.

70. John Vidal, 'Biotech Food Giant Wields Power in Washington', *The Guardian*, 18 February 1999, p. 8.

71. John Vidal, 'Food Firm's PR Errors,' The Guardian April 13, 1998.

72. Sarah Hall, 'Monsanto Ads Condemned', *The Guardian*, 1 March 1999, page 5.

73. Jeremy Rifkins, *The Biotech Century*, 1998, London: Victor Gollancz.

74. James, Meikle, 'Gene-modified products barred from health food stores', *The Guardian*, June 24, 1998.

75. Geoffrey Lean, 'The Humbling of a GM Giant", *The Independent*, 4 October 1999, p. 18.

76. Julian Borger, 'US Growers Join the Backlash as Prices Tumble', *The Guardian*, 5 October 1999, p. 14.

77. 'Revolt of the Food Experts', *Healthy Living*, Spring, 1999, p. 6.

78. Michael Hegarty, "Too Much Haste" to Genetic Plants,' *Farming Independent*, 24 March 1998, p. 3.

79. Mae-Wan Ho, 'The Unholy Alliance', *The Ecologist*, July/August 1997, pp., 152-158.

80. 'National Consultation Debate on Genetically Modified Organisms and the Environment', Department of the Environment, Dublin, 28 July, 1999.

81. Geoffrey Lean, 'Labour Sues for Peace on GM Foods', *The Independent on Sunday*, October 10, 1999, p. 6.

CHAPTER 7

Eucharist Renewing theCovenant

1. *The Catechism of the Catholic Church*, 1994, Dublin, Veritas Publications.

2. David, N. Power, *The Eucharistic Mystery: Revitalizing the Tradition*, 1992, Dublin, Gill and Macmillan, Dublin, p. 9.

3. Ibid. p. 5.

4. Ibid. p. 74.

5. Robert Murray, *The Cosmic Covenant*, 1992, London, Heythrop Monograph, Sheed and Ward, p. 93.

6. Edward O. Wilson, *The Diversity of Life*, 1993, Harmondsworth, Penguin Books, p. 268.

7. Louke van Wensveen Sider, 'The Seven Deadly Sins in an Ecological Age', unpublished.

8. Gregory Dix, *The Shape of The Liturgy*, 1945, London, Dacre Press, Adam and Charles Black, p. 115.

9. Dix, op. cit., p. 50. According to Dix 'the type of meal to which it best conforms is the formal supper of a chaburah [from chaber, a friend].'

10. Dix, op. cit., page 115.

11. Dix, op. cit., p. 157: 'Hippolytus's prayer runs thus: "We render thanks unto Thee, O God, through Thy Beloved Servant Jesus Christ, Whom in the last times thou didst send (to be) a Saviour and Redeemer and the Angel of Thy counsel; Who is Thy Word inseparable (from Thee); through Whom Thou madest all things, and in Whom Thou wast well-pleased".'

12. Brian Swimme and Thomas Berry, *The Universe Story*, 1992, Harper San Francisco.

13. Richard N. Fragomeni, 'Liturgy at the Heart of Creation: Towards an Ecological Consciousness in Prayer' in *The Ecological Challenge* (ed. Ricard N. Fragomeni and John T. Pawlikski) 1994, Collegeville, Liturgical Press, p. 67.

14. Jay B. McDaniel, *With Roots and Wings*, 1995, Maryknoll, Orbis Books, pp. 75-113.

15. Barbara Sproul, *Primal Myths*, 1979, London, Harper and Row, p. 331.

16. Mike Samuels and Hal Zina Bennett, *Well Body, Well Earth*, 1983, San Francisco, Sierra Club Books, p. 18.

17. David Power, op. cit., p. 295.